Notes from the
Languedoc

Notes from the
Languedoc

RUPERT WRIGHT

EBURY
PRESS

First published by Domens in France 2003

This edition published by Ebury Press in Great Britain in 2005

10

Ebury Press
Random House, 20 Vauxhall Bridge Road, London SW1V 2SA

Addresses for companies within The Random House Group can be found at: www.randomhouse.co.uk

The Random House Group Limited Reg. No. 954009

www.randomhouse.co.uk

A CIP catalogue record for this book is available from the British Library

Cover Design by Two Associated
Text design and typesetting by Textype

ISBN 9780091905637

The Random House Group Limited supports The Forest Stewardship Council® (FSC®), the leading international forest-certification organisation. Our books carrying the FSC label are printed on FSC®-certified paper. FSC is the only forest-certification scheme supported by the leading environmental organisations, including Greenpeace. Our paper procurement policy can be found at www.randomhouse.co.uk/environment

MIX
Paper from
responsible sources
FSC® C016897

Printed and bound in Great Britain by Clays Ltd, St Ives plc

Note

These letters were originally written for my grandmother, Kitty. I have edited them a little, and taken out some unnecessary biographical details. I have also added a couple of extracts from letters written to my son, Hugo, happily incarcerated in an English boarding school. There are also a number of passages that first appeared in the *Financial Times* and the *Sunday Times*.

R.A.J.W.

Sainte Cécile, Languedoc, 2005

PREFACE

It is easy to get to the Languedoc. All you have to do is drive down the Rhône valley until you reach the Mediterranean coast, then turn right. However, the mystery is that for generations most people have been turning left in the direction of Italy. Go into any bookshop, and you will find 20 books on Provence. About its neighbour, the Languedoc, you will be lucky to find a map and possibly a Michelin guide. Even when people did turn right, they would normally drive straight through it to Spain. Sometimes they stopped, but didn't linger. They came for a week in the sun, and returned home with sunburn and a carafe of thin wine.

This book aims to correct that imbalance, for there is much to enjoy in the Languedoc: it is a land of castles and heretics, vineyards and scented hillsides, boar hunts and bullfights, canals and oyster beds, flamingos and sandy beaches. Throughout it all rages a strong wind, most noticeable when it is absent. Best of all are the people: noisy, nosy, loyal, friendly to strangers unless you come from Paris, and fiercely proud of their customs and countryside, even if they usually drive too fast to appreciate it.

This is an account of three years exploring a small part of this great area. I have hardly ventured into Roussillon, except to visit some of its castles and a bit of its coastline; much of the High Languedoc remains a mystery to me. I apologise in advance to fans of those areas. Maybe one day I will get around to visiting them, or better still perhaps, somebody else will. I have visited some of the best places within a 75-kilometre radius of Pézenas, a small market town half an hour from both the Mediterranean coast and Montpellier, as well as recounting some of the history that makes this area so special.

Critics may, among its other faults, accuse this book of lacking narrative drive. This at least is deliberate: it is designed to ramble, to be discursive, because this is how I feel the Languedoc can best be discovered. Get yourself lost in the Languedoc, and you will find much to enjoy in the process.

Many people have played a hand in introducing me to the delights of the place, too many to mention them all, but I should single out a few without whom this book would be much poorer: Peter Glynn Smith and his wife Dominique – if I hadn't met them on a boat in Thailand I would never have come here in the first place; Jean-Claude Mas, who tried to educate my palate, and introduce me to many wines of the region; Jean-Luc Clerc, who tempted me with delicacies from his shop and showed a stoicism normally reserved for Roman emperors; Caroline Mascou, who helped me drive to some of the places, got us stuck on a sandbar, but more importantly, managed to get us off; Nick Chadwick, who lent me his powder-blue Jaguar, so that everywhere I went I was treated like a visiting milord; Ella Fallgren; John Hinton, who agreed to work on this project even though he has worked with me before and should know better; all the winemakers and shopkeepers and bar owners and cyclists who answered my questions; and above all Helena, who agreed to leave England and move to a part of France she had never heard of. This book is for her.

LETTERS

Sainte Cécile, August 2000

In the shade of a fig tree – the dog wants a walk –
the landscape of the Languedoc – our nights are like
your days – a forgotten land, filled with the sound
of lutes – northern man flies south – meeting a Jesuit
priest – the local village – a bottle of wine

I AM WRITING THIS LETTER in the shade of a fig tree. It is eight o'clock in the evening, but it is still too hot to sit in the sun. Besides, I like this fig tree. Its leaves are like the gloves of a five-fingered, green giant. They shine as if they have just been polished. I recall that in literature, the English use the leaf of a fig tree to cover their modesty; the French make do with a vine leaf. Is this anything to do with size, or just a question of convenience? Either way, there is no need for any covering up here. I could wander round the garden naked as Adam if I chose. The only living creatures that would notice are the birds that fly overhead.

I have now been in the house for a week. Tomorrow the family arrives. There will be suitcases, discarded teddy bears and screams from the swimming pool. This is how

1

it should be. A house like this should be filled with children. I look forward to their arrival. But I confess that I have had a good time on my own.

Not that I have achieved as much as I might have done. For example, at last I now have more shelf space than books. The old lady that lived here had a huge collection. It is said that she read one new book in the morning and another in the afternoon. Her copies of Molière, Camus and Françoise Sagan have been packed up and taken away. Still sitting in their boxes are my books, including dog-eared copies of Shakespeare, Hemingway and Carl Hiaasen. They can wait.

I have spent a lot of time in a rocking chair on the terrace, looking at the countryside. When I came here in May the road side and much of the hills were covered in wild flowers, cistus, lavender, fennel, rosemary and thyme. The smell was so strong that you could almost marinade a leg of lamb by exposing it to the air. Now the colours and the flowers have gone. It is almost as if the sun has sucked the countryside dry, leaving the ground hard and the colours reduced to a monochrome. The effect is almost more beautiful, in the way that a black and white photograph can sometimes be better than a colour image.

What remains are the trees and plants that are designed to withstand this solar assault. This includes the pine trees at the base of the hill opposite. There is a small stream that runs at the foot of the hill. Although it has long dried up, an assortment of bushes grow up on its banks, including what looks like a giant stand of bamboo. I am told it is cannisse, a plant indigenous to the region. Before I learnt this, I had visions of a Chinese connection, with planting taking place throughout the south to feed a colony of giant pandas given to Louis XIV as a wedding present. Alas, that proved to be idle speculation.

Beyond the river bank is an olive grove. The trunks are twisted with age, their leaves a two-tone green, dark on top and light underneath. It is surely the loveliest of trees. A better place to sit and stare at the sky cannot be imagined. Past the olives the vines begin. They seem to grow on just rocks. Even at night the ground radiates heat. But the leaves are still thick and green. The roots must stretch to the very centre of the earth to find moisture. Hidden in the branches are clusters of grapes, but I have never seen so many! It is not unusual to see six, seven, eight or more big bunches hanging pendulously from the branches. I amuse myself by counting how many bottles one could get from the view, but the task is daunting, and beyond my grasp of mathematics.

The terrace faces due south. I can be in my rocking chair at seven in the morning, when it is still cool. But once the sun appears over the hill to the east, the heat begins. If I could bear to look at the sun I could follow its path through the burning sky. Once this week a cloud dared to pass in front, momentarily darkening it. On another occasion two kites wheeled in front, as if seeking to surprise their prey like a German fighter ace. But otherwise the sun has been unrelenting and unchallenged.

Now, at last, the shadows are lengthening. Trees on the hill are throwing up giant images. The small outcrop of rock has become a palace. We are perched on the foothills of the mountains that will march up via various plateaux to the Massif Central. As you get further north and higher, there is more garrigue. This is the name they give to the wild country here, that is dominated by a small, dark green holm oak tree. In these depths live wild boars, with tusks that can slice a dog in half.

The dog here – an Alsatian left by the previous owners – seems unaffected by the danger he faces. I think he would like me to be more energetic. Watching me watching the countryside does not seem to be his idea of fun. Most of the day he lies beside me under the fig tree. When he hears me move to get a glass of water, he stretches expectantly, only to sink back in disappointment.

This afternoon I decided to take him for a walk. It was so hot that even the cicadas were momentarily stilled. Most days they keep up an incessant clatter, a noise created by their abdomens to attract a mate. At ten o'clock at night, exactly, they go silent, as if controlled by a watchmaker.

We followed the road that leads past the house towards the small vineyard at the back. Here there are four small parcels of vines. The white grapes have already been picked. A bunch that has fallen from the trailer is lying on the ground, burst and smelling honey sweet. The red grapes will be picked any day now. I pick a small bunch and taste them. They are ripe and ready and taste good, even though they are produced for wine making. I throw some for the dog. They are sticky.

There are a couple of small huts up here. In the Languedoc a farmhouse is called a mas. These little houses are called mazets. They were built in the days before the car made it possible to run back home for lunch. Here, in these small shelters, workers would keep their implements, share a bottle of wine with their friends, and take afternoon siestas. There are fruit trees growing nearby, offering shade and fruit in season. These mazets are dotted throughout this large land. Those near the roadside are often covered in painted advertisements for forgotten drinks or shops that no longer exist. Many of them are falling down. Soon, when all their roofs have caved in, they will be useful only to archaeologists, who will recall in them something from the Stone Age.

The road becomes a narrow track, used only by hunters judging from the spent cartridges that litter the route. It winds up to the top of the hill, about 200 metres above sea level. From here there is a good view of the house. It is built of stone, with large buttresses like a Gothic cathedral, to stop the walls from falling in. Parts of the house date from the 18th century. It is thought that there used to be a church here. Then it became a farm, and was enlarged to keep the farmer's family, his goats and a cellar to make wine. The tiles on the roof are red; the shutters bright blue. There are lemon trees growing in pots, wisteria on the terrace and ivy growing on the walls. There is a large palm tree at the end of the terrace, which waves its arms in the wind like a semaphoring soldier. In the garden there are acacia trees, an almond tree, and a couple of agaves, rather splendid-looking light blue and green plants, with sharp tips. It is said you can make tequila from them. Best of all are the jasmine and honeysuckle plants, which in the evening fill the air with a scent of exotic call girls.

I like the exterior of the house. Not much will need changing. Inside it is a different matter. The owner's son was an architect. Clearly under the spell of Le Corbusier, he committed some dreadful crimes in the name of Modernism. There is an atrium between the ground and the first floor. Surrounding the hole is a blue metal balustrade, the sort of thing you might expect to find on a ferry to stop yourself from pitching into the Channel. There is a big blue column, designed no doubt to keep the roof from caving in. The doors are flimsy, apparently made of nothing better than cardboard, that bang shut on the slightest breeze. And there is garish blue paint everywhere. You would think that Yves Klein had lived here. It will have to go.

But there is time. From where the dog and I are

standing, you can look beyond the house. There are two round hills, covered in short, dark green oak trees. They look as if they have been like that forever. Beyond them is a flat plain, where vines grow. Bursting out of one vineyard is a large outcrop of rocks, nearly 100 metres high, with a plateau on top. If this were in Provence, it would be a famous picnic spot. Cézanne would have painted it. Picasso would have made love on it. Fortunately, we are not in Provence. Beyond the plain, the ground begins to rise. Half way in the distance sits a small village. And beyond that, the hills rise in succession, one after another until they reach the first mountain, a hazy blue, with a cross on top.

When it's dark the village lights make it look like a familiar constellation. Night is when I normally walk the dog. This week there has been no moon, so the stars have been spectacular. Only in Africa have I seen so many stars. It is intoxicating. No wonder Racine boasted to his friends in the north that 'our nights are like your days'. Looking down, there are even little constellations by the path. They are made by glow worms, tiny beetles that emit a green light. When I shine a torch on them, they turn dim, as if embarrassed to be outpowered.

At night from the top of this hill there are just the lights of the little village and beyond, those of Faugères. It is a famous wine-making village, but there is little reason to visit it. Except for these two places, there is nothing but darkness. When the wind blows, it is like being on a ship, with just the lights of a couple of ports in the distance.

Turning south, the vines continue their march towards the Mediterranean. A butterfly that lived off vine leaves could make its erratic way – with a favourable north wind – over that last hill with the rocky outcrop, alongside the plane trees that line the road, around the medieval town of Pézenas and on to the sea itself.

Why am I drawn to this landscape, so different from the tall oaks and green fields of Sussex that you and I know so well? This is a violent land, of extreme rainfall followed by drought. There is a searing wind that blows from the north, bringing good weather. When it blows from the south, it brings mist or sandy rain from the Sahara. There is nothing mean or dishonest, no drizzle. Everything is raw and exposed, not hidden or hypo-critical. This is what I love. Seen from my rocking chair, England seems a long way away, its squabbles petty, its people concerned only with making money and complaining about the weather. I feel rather like an astronaut, peering from his spaceship, who covers the world and all its problems with his thumb.

The Languedoc, until recently, was as remote as a space station, if perhaps more accessible. The Phoenicians and Greeks came in their ships. The Romans marched like tortoises and built a mighty road along the coast. At the end of the first millennium, the Languedoc was one of the most civilised places in Europe. The Franks and the

Visigoths came following the sack of Rome, while the Saracens made a brief foray lasting 40 years until they were turned back in Poitiers and eventually pushed back to Spain and finally Africa.

By all accounts, it was a fine place to live in those times. The air was filled with the sound of lutes and singing troubadours. But the crusade against the Cathars at the beginning of the 13th century replaced the music with cries of pain. France was united, but the south was left bitter and gradually forgotten. Rain in the winter made the roads impassable. Even the Roman road along the coast became unusable, the bridges were washed away by the floods and not replaced, and mosquitoes bred in the swamps caused by the receding sea. A canal was built in the 1600s to link the Atlantic with the Mediterranean, but apart from sending rich wine to boost the thin stuff produced by Bordeaux, and making a few individuals quite wealthy, there was little benefit to the region.

As you know, the English invented the Côte d'Azur at the beginning of the 1900s, but rarely ventured west of the Rhône. A few artists came, painted, and returned to Paris to sell their work. By then a few land owners had become spectacularly rich from making wine, and later, went even more spectacularly broke. In the end it was left to the European Community to soak up the wine lake and pay people to pull up their vines. In the 1960s and 1970s a few adventurers came and liked what they saw, but it was still as remote as Kathmandu, with fewer visitors.

Life for the locals was tough, but good. There was always an abundance of food. There was fish from the sea and the lagoons, and two crops of fruit a year. This is why the Romans called one of their cities Béziers – literally Bi-terroirs, or 'Two crops'.

(I put down my pen a moment ago and picked one of the purple figs. I like the colour and the taste, even if the autumn crop is not as juicy as those I remember from May.)

It seems though that now, at the beginning of the 21st century, I am not alone in discovering this place. People are no longer charging through to visit Spain, but stopping, and buying houses. New airlines have opened up flights to Montpellier, Carcassonne, Nîmes and Perpignan. Every plane brings a load of pale faces wearing shorts and sandals, desperate for a place in the sun.

The French are coming too. They are fleeing the rain in the north and moving south for the good life. While the English and the Dutch and the Germans are buying the old houses and renovating them, the French are buying small houses on new developments. Each village has a ring of them on the outskirts like a nasty rash. But soon the sun will bleach the houses so they look less offensive.

The sun has nearly gone now. Soon I shall be able to come out from the shade of the fig tree and have something to eat. Today it was market day in the little village at the foot of the valley. I walked the four kilometres down the hill, along the winding road that crosses the river twice as it too wanders towards the sea. I met only one person on the way, an old priest with a hat and a cane. He tipped his hat to me as I passed, so we talked for a while. He was a Jesuit, now retired. 'The beauty of the valley of the Hérault on mornings like these is proof surely of the existence of God,' he said.

From the bridge there is a good view of the houses, which are typical of the region. Although many of the villages claim a thousand years of history, and many of the castles and churches date from around that time, most of the houses date from the 19th century. They are quite large, two or three storeys, with shuttered windows and stuccoed walls. On the ground floor there is a doorway and a large garage, often with a curved entrance. Inside these garages is where everyone used to make their own wine, one hundred years before the garage wine makers of St Emilion. Still today they house the tractors and trailers and essential tools for looking after vines. The only sign of ornament or frippery comes in the form of the railings on the balconies. Most are quite plain, but some are heavily decorated, while others have a definite touch of Art Deco.

In the middle of the village, a number of vans had been set up around the fountain. It is curious that in this land where water is so important, each village has its own fountain, trickling away day and night. I am reminded of the mosques in the Middle East, many of which were built on the site of springs. Water and God are closely linked in dry lands.

And what of the people? They seem friendly enough. They speak a heavily accented French, as far from Parisian French as a West Country drawl is from BBC English. It is only in the last hundred years or so that they have started to speak French. Before then the common language was Occitan. While French was used for official documents, Occitan was the language of the village. There are still a number of the older people who speak it, even though it was banned in the schools.

They have one curious habit. In the early evenings, until late at night, they come out of their houses and sit in the streets. They watch the cars and chat to each other, but the sexes are strictly segregated. There is a group of women that gathers in the newly built bus shelter, huddled under a giant painted Dubonnet poster that is gradually fading from view. The men seem to have colonised the area under the plane trees beside the fountain. If there is not enough space on the seats or benches, they bring deck chairs. I guess it beats watching television.

I bought tomatoes and melon, ham and pâté in the local shop, and a mountain cheese called Cantal, which is made not far away. It is rather like Cheddar, but with a creamier consistency. I also bought a loaf of bread from the bakery. These ingredients will be the basis of a good dinner. I might even open a bottle of the wine that the woodman brought me. I met him earlier this week. He was clearing a path on the hill. I went over to him and we chattted for a while. He is about 50, with a large nose, a pipe, and lines around his eyes, creased by the sun. Despite the heat, he was wearing a jacket and a hat.

'You're not from round here,' he said.
'No.'
'Are you from Paris?'
'No. London.'
'Thank God. I hate Parisians.'
Earlier today I heard his van drive up to the house and stop. I went out to stop the dog barking and offered him a cup of coffee. He pulled out an unlabelled bottle of wine from his jacket.

'This is for you,' he said. 'It's a bottle of wine made from Carignan grapes. Welcome to the Languedoc.'

When will you come and visit? I am sure you will find much to amuse and delight you. But I should wait until the children have gone and the tourists have returned to their offices. And then we can have some fun. In the meantime, I must go now and eat my bread and cheese, and, perhaps, drink a small glass of wine.

On a vineyard, September 2000

Red roses, red grapes – new winemakers revive region – Greeks come bearing amphorae – the Romans start planting vines – wine is life

 HAVE JUST RETURNED FROM a walk in the vineyards. It is seven o'clock in the morning, but the sun is up and the picking season is in full swing. I thought of you as I walked past a row of vines with rose bushes at the end. The roses are no longer in full bloom, withered by the Midi sun, but still red. But why do you think a winemaker would bother to plant roses? As presents for his mistresses? Possibly. But also because vines and roses catch many of the same diseases, especially mildew. Just as miners take canaries down into their mines because they are more susceptible to gases, so winemakers grow roses because they show the early symptoms of disease. Keep an eye on your roses, and you can keep your vines healthy. That's the theory anyway. At least it makes for a pretty walk.

As I may have mentioned before, wine dominates this

area more than any other region in France. It stretches from the mouth of the Rhône to the foothills of the Pyrenees, making it the biggest vineyard in the world. And the wine trade is the most important business in the Languedoc – perhaps the only industry, although tourism is catching up. People either own vineyards, blend wine, pick grapes, market wine or sell it. At our village school the children even have their own vineyard, where they make their own wine, a tasty blend of Grenache and Carignan. The landscape is dominated by rows of cultivated vines. Huge tracts of hillside are carved out by bulldozers, then planted with tiny vines. When the autumn comes and the leaves begin to change colour, the reds and yellows and oranges are a sight to match the beauty of the New England fall.

Vines are everywhere. They cling to the coast of the Etang de Thau, overlooking the oyster beds. They stretch up into the hills, planted on steep slopes where only goats graze and the grapes have to be moved by hand or with the help of tracked machines. Sometimes they are in huge fields, cut like the maze hedges of Hampton Court. In Saint-Chinian there is even a roundabout with a vineyard in the middle. I don't know if they harvest the grapes or leave them to wither on the vine, but it makes a change from the usual clump of lavender. On the outskirts of villages, new houses are being built in vineyards. The developer takes just as much land as is needed for the building, leaving a number of vines still standing, as if it would be unlucky to uproot too many of them. This makes for strange gardens, but nobody seems to mind.

The history of wine in the Languedoc has been one of short periods of boom and prosperity, followed by long years of attrition and penury. It has forced the growers of grapes into co-operatives, huddled together for their own security. It has led to rebellion, revolt, deaths. While the co-operatives make up 70 per cent of all the wine produced in the Languedoc, people do not want to drink cheap wine any more. They would prefer to drink better wine.

A bewildering number of styles of wine are produced here. From Limoux in the west comes a sparkling wine that they claim was first produced in 1531, a hundred years before the monk Dom Pérignon discovered how to make champagne. Above Montpellier are the winemakers of Pic St Loup, who produce elegant red wines. Further west, and closer to us, is the appellation of Faugères. The land is higher – up to 250 metres above sea level. The poor soil – lots of rocky schist – makes the vine work hard for its fruit.

It is an obvious but often overlooked fact that to produce good wine you need to start with good grapes. Vines grown on hillsides tend to produce better grapes, full of taste and character. Their roots stretch down into the soil, struggling to get enough moisture. The wines of Faugères, such as Domaine du Météore, Domaine Ollier

Taillefer or Château des Estanilles, are rich in colour, almost purple, with an elegant nose and a taste of wild fruits. Further west lies Saint-Chinian. I can never drive past the small village or see its label without imagining schoolgirls with hockey sticks, screaming furiously. Its wines are equally difficult to ignore, although they can be of variable quality. Canet Valette is one that I seek out on a wine list. It is powerful and seductive. Best of all from Saint-Chinian is the wine from Clos Bagatelle, packed with fruit and taste.

Further west is Fitou. I regret to say that I have not had a decent Fitou since I have been in France. Perhaps they send all the best bottles to London. Then there are the country wines of Minervois and Corbières, many of which are improving quickly. People from Béziers regard this area as backward and full of peasants, but a number of British investors, such as Graham Nutter, an investment banker, and John Hegarty, an advertising man, are spending thousands of pounds on vineyards, new equipment and marketing.

The region's wine revival began in the 1980s, when visiting wine makers flew in from Australia and other parts of the New World. They quickly realised that here were all the ingredients for making good wines. New technology was introduced. The picking of the best white grapes was done at night to prevent oxidation. Some of the old vines – such as Carignan and Aramon, which were grown mainly for the sheer quantity of wine that they produced – were uprooted and replaced with Cabernet Sauvignon, Syrah and Chardonnay. Cleanliness and hygiene were insisted on. And gradually New World wine techniques transformed the Old World's oldest vineyards. Among its numerous wine makers are a plethora of wine stars – including Jean-Luc Colombo, a charismatic wine maker with estates in the Rhône and the Languedoc; Jean-Claude Mas, who produces a stunning blend of Chardonnay and Viognier near Pézenas; and Catherine Roque, who defies convention and the authorities and grows Pinot Noir, the grape of red Burgundy, on the hills above Bédarieux.

Part of the joy for a wine drinker is the delight in discovering a new fine-tasting bottle. Of the wines in the region, these are the ones we drink most: Clos Bagatelle, Domaine de l'Hortus, Château Paul Mas, Domaine de l'Arjolle; Domaine la Voulte-Gasparets; Cante Perdrix; Château de Jonquières; Domaine Canet Valette; Château Coujan and anything else we can get our hands on. I am sure many of these are now available in London.

It is generally accepted that the man who first saw and exploited the potential of the Languedoc as an area to make great wine is Aimé Guibert. His wine, Mas de Daumas Gassac, was drunk by Bill Clinton and Tony Blair at a dinner in 10 Downing Street.

Guibert, a member of a famous glove-making family, bought an estate near Aniane in 1970. With the help of Emile Peynaud, a wine consultant, Guibert and his wife

Véronique transformed the garrigue into a vineyard, with grape varieties that were then rare in the region, including Cabernet Sauvignon, Cabernet Franc, Syrah, Merlot, Viognier, Chardonnay, and Petit Manseng. With good contacts in the fashion industry, he managed to create a buzz about his wines, which he began to sell for incredible prices.

Guibert looks the sort of man who would make elegant, cultivated wine. He is well educated, a lover of opera, with a shock of grey hair and blue eyes. He impressed me when we met at a dinner party by asking for a glass of whisky, turning down the offer of a glass of wine. He then went on to tell me that the English were the only people who really appreciated wine. 'From 1550 to 1950 it was only the English families who understood and who drank wine,' he said. 'The French are just catching up, but they have a long way to go.'

Despite the wine-making stars, there is still a lot of over-capacity in the industry. Many of the co-operatives are bankrupt, badly managed by their members and now up for sale. One of the first co-operatives in France was set up in Maraussan, close to Béziers, in 1901, but most of them date from the 1930s. In some areas near Nîmes they are converting the wine-making buildings into holiday apartments. The co-operatives were set up primarily for the benefit of their members, not the consumers. It is still considered the fault of somebody else – the government, normally – when there is a problem of oversupply due to a lack of demand.

To some extent the industry has not adapted to the change in the market. It is now possible to buy perfectly good wine from Australia, North America, South America, South Africa, and even some parts of eastern Europe. While the Languedoc has struggled for acceptance among a generation of drinkers in France who think that Bordeaux and Burgundy offer better quality, it has lost out on many new opportunities. There are some growers who know that it is not enough simply to make wine, you have to sell it too, but in the main, many producers still find it inexplicable that people might choose to buy a bottle of wine that tells you what kind of grape you are drinking.

And there are still some dubious practices. For example, it takes up to 10 years for a vineyard to become productive, although you can produce wine after three years. Even so, the wine growers of the Languedoc managed to double the production of Merlot between 1996 and 1998. How did they achieve this alchemy? According to some sources, they substituted Aramon for Merlot. Aramon is a noble grape variety, much loved in Spain, but it is not Merlot. However, there is no chemical test that can determine the exact nature of the grape. If the wine in the bottle tastes like the grape it is supposed to be, you have no way of knowing whether the wine maker is lying.

In the 19th century there was a bestselling book that told people how to make wine out of raisins. There is the story of the local winegrower who, after explaining to his son all his methods and techniques for making wine, says: 'And don't forget son. You can also make wine from grapes.'

Vines have been cultivated in the Midi since the time of the Greeks, five centuries before Christ, according to the *Guide Hachette*, the wine bible, which holds an annual blind tasting and selects its favourite wines. But one night Jean-Pierre, local historian and wine maker, who helps me in the garden, was keeping his wife company while she was babysitting the children. He spent the evening reading my *Guide Hachette* and wrote the following correction in its pages: 'Wine was cultivated in the first century before Christ by the Romans in the Languedoc. Between the 6th and 2nd centuries before Christ, wine was transported by the Greeks and Romans in amphorae. During this period there were no cultivated vines in the Languedoc.'

At least all the authorities agree that the Languedoc is the oldest wine-growing area in France. Bordeaux in contrast did not get round to making wine until hundreds of years later. The Romans were thirsty and energetic. They shipped wine from the Languedoc throughout the Roman Empire. Pliny the Younger was so impressed by the wine of Béziers that he kept an amphora from the region and did not drink it for five years. Either that, or he put it away in his cellar, only drinking it one night in desperation when there was nothing else to hand, or he wanted to get rid of some unwanted guests. Cicero was another Roman to praise the Midi wines. It is refreshing to imagine the great orator sitting in the shade of a mulberry tree, nursing a glass of Languedoc wine and planning his next Philippic.

As well as growing and making the wine, each estate would have its own amphora-making operation, rather like an onsite pottery. Amphora is a Latin word from the Greek for a vessel with two handles. They are made of clay and come in different sizes: those used for storing and shipping olive oil tended to be wider in the beam; wine amphorae were narrow, often with a pointed bottom, which helped in the pouring but must have made them a bugger to balance after a few drinks. They were stored in the holds of the ships and held together by metal bars that went through the handles. An amphora holds about 25 litres of wine. The Romans were either able to consume considerable quantities of wine or were not too worried about the state of the wine when they did. Nowadays there are mobile bottling plants that come on the back of large lorries. They park by the side of the road and can fill and cork hundreds of bottles in an hour.

During Trimalchio's banquet in Petronius's *Satyricon*, the host turns to his guests and declares that 'Wine is life'. But what kind of wine or life was it? One assumes they liked their wines rich, strong and plentiful. But as for quality, it is hard to imagine that they were able to keep the wine in sufficiently good condition to age it. It was Louis Pasteur, many centuries later, who recognised that it was the effect of air on wine that contributed to it turning to vinegar. The Romans are unlikely to have been able to keep the wine from oxidising for long. Columella, a Roman author who wrote a large treatise on wine, says that wine without added preservatives tastes better. As chalk or marble dust was often added to offset acidity, one can only agree with him. There are also reports of adding sea water or salt to wine during fermentation. The Romans were at least aware of the benefits of ageing wine. Under Roman law, the distinction between new and old wine was one year. Fears of a European wine lake existed even in Roman times. In AD 92, the emperor Domitian ordered half the vines in the Languedoc to be pulled up. This decree was not overturned until 270 by the emperor Probus.

After the decline of the Roman Empire it was left to the monasteries to keep the tradition of vine cultivation alive. The use of wine in the Eucharist, its symbolic role as the blood of Christ, comes from the Jewish religion. However, although the monasteries ended up in control of many of the vineyards in this period, this may be more to do with economic power than the need to cultivate wine specifically for the Eucharist. Many of the monasteries and vineyards were the result of grants or favours from royalty or nobles, hoping for preferential treatment in the afterlife. The monks travelled with their grapes, planting as they converted. The Dominicans probably brought Pinot Noir to the Languedoc, although now it is only grown in a few isolated places. This is probably the only decent thing they ever did.

Sommières, Christmas 2000

A dog called Tintin – Molière comes to Pézenas – an
owl in a windmill – acting the goat – going to Lamalou
– a tomb by the sea – Durrell's purple prose and face –
Hemingway in the Camargue – Blixen in Lunel – a
man hides in Collioure and changes his name – a
Frenchman plans a book on Sussex

MERRY CHRISTMAS. TODAY IT is raining, wild furious
rain, filling the ditches and pouring off the roofs.
There is no possibility of a walk today. I am holed up in a
little café in Sommières, a small village in the Gard. There
is nobody here but a bored bar owner and a dog called
Tintin. The man is drinking pastis and the dog is walking
up and down the bar like a condemned prisoner in a cell.

I thought I would write to you. What would you like to
hear about apart from the weather? What about the
writers of the Languedoc? It is an ideal location for
writers. Here there is everything you might need: cheap
housing, plentiful wine and food, sunshine (except
today), the companionship of friends and plenty of
distractions to keep you from your desk.

It was the French writers who first discovered Pézenas. Molière came, not for the climate or the seafood, but because he was banished from Paris because of something he had written. He moved south in search of work, and found it in Pézenas. He was born Jean-Baptiste Poquelin, of fairly humble origins. His father was an upholsterer. He was educated by Jesuits. At 16 he went to Orléans to study law, but abandoned it in favour of acting and the theatre. When he failed in Paris he found a patron in the Prince of Conti.

In Pézenas Molière produced *The Jealous Husband* and *The Misanthrope*. There is a plaque on a wall in the Place Gambetta, saying that this was the site of Barbier Gely's shop. Molière was friends with the barber, and used to pick up ideas for plots from the conversation of his clients. But he did not stay more than a few summers in Pézenas. His patron grew misanthropic, turning against the theatre in 1657 to lead a devout life and pursuing its players with all the passion of a convert.

Molière and his men moved back to Paris, where this time they managed to win favour at the court, in particular with the king's brother. This was Molière's golden age. Louis XIV was made godfather to his first son. He wrote a string of plays, including *Tartuffe*, but he fell seriously ill and was put on a diet of milk. After something of a recovery, he wrote and insisted on starring in *The Hypochondriac*. On just the fourth performance he collapsed on stage, was taken home and died. His widow,

Armande, had to gain the support of Louis XIV and the Archbishop of Paris to allow him a proper burial, a right that most actors forfeited by their choice of profession. I find myself unmoved by Molière. In fact, even worse, I find him unreadable. Everyone has a dark secret and here is one of mine. I have never managed to get past the first page with Molière. A number of his plays are staged during the summer months during the Mirondela festival of arts in Pézenas. One day I may even go to one.

Another Frenchman, Alphonse Daudet, was born in Nîmes nearly 250 years later in 1840. When he was eight he moved to Lyons following the death of his father. After school he followed his elder brother to Paris, where he found work as a journalist on *Le Figaro*, and became secretary to the Duc de Mornay. This occupation was clearly quite relaxing, for he found plenty of time to write and to make friends with people such as Emile Zola and Frédéric Mistral. Mistral is a relatively unknown and certainly unread author these days, but he used to be popular. He grew up in the south of France, but chose to write in the Provençal language, a close relative of the Langue d'Oc. This enchanted the Swedish Nobel Prize committee, but leaves most readers perplexed and none the wiser these days.

He shares his name with the wind that whistles down the Rhône, which sends expatriates mad in the winter. Elizabeth David, the English cook and writer who probably did more than anyone to publicise the charms of Provence in the period after the Second World War, wrote: 'One winter and spring when the mistral never ceased its relentless screaming round our crumbling hill village opposite the Lubéron mountain, we all seemed to come perilously close to losing our reason, although it is, of course, only fair to say that the truly awful wine of that particular district no doubt also contributed its share.'

Daudet wrote in French. He is still celebrated, and read, for one main work, *Lettres de Mon Moulin*, which was published in 1869. Tired of Parisian life, the narrator retires to a windmill in the south of France, near the village of Fontvielle. He shares his lodging with an owl. His friends are farmers, particularly Cornille the miller, who is being put out of business by the new steam mills.

You can still visit his windmill or, rather, you can visit a windmill that claims to be the place where he stayed. It is more likely to be the real windmill than the one in Spain that Japanese tourists are told was attacked by Don Quixote. But if you follow the signs in Fontvielle you come to a car park and a track that leads you to a small round building on a hill, with a cone like a witch's hat on the top and arms where the sails would have been. There is a stuffed owl in the roof. You can buy Daudet's books in the basement. I bought an attractive copy of *Lettres de Mon Moulin*, and sat in the shade of an olive tree to read it. He writes well. He describes the rabbits who are surprised at his arrival, his lodger the owl, the sunshine, the pine trees, the Alpilles in the distance, the silence and, far away, the sound of a fife, a curlew in the lavender, mule bells on the road.

I was delighted to learn later that Daudet did not put himself through too much country living to write this book, lyrical as it is. Thoreau he was not. He did not really stay in a mill. You could not expect a Parisian writer to share his bedroom with an owl. Instead he stayed at the château down the road, where he slept in linen sheets, drank fine wines and flirted with the chambermaids. Maybe he disturbed the rabbits on an evening walk, or listened to the silence after a good lunch at the château.

Daudet is best known for one of the stories in the book called *The Goat of Monsieur Seguin*. It is beloved of French schoolchildren, who read it soon after Saint-Exupéry's *Le Petit Prince*. It is addressed to a certain Pierre Gringoire, a lyric poet in Paris. It tells the story of a small goat that lives in the countryside with a farmer called Monsieur Seguin. The goat wants to be free. The farmer has never had any luck with his goats. They run away to the hills, where they get eaten by a wolf. The goat, whose name is Blanquette, pleads with the farmer to be allowed to go to the mountains.

'What will you do if you meet the wolf?' asks the farmer. 'Hit him with my horns,' says the goat. 'Ha,' says the farmer. 'The wolf will laugh at your horns. He has eaten animals with bigger horns than you. Remember Renaude who was here last year? She was strong and naughty as a billy goat. She fought with the wolf all night long. Then, in the morning, he ate her.'

Instead the farmer puts her up in a dark stable and double locks the door. But the white goat escapes through the window and runs away. 'You're laughing, hey Gringoire,' writes Daudet. 'You're on the side of the goats against the good Monsieur Seguin. We will see if you are laughing later.'

When the goat gets to the mountain, everything is splendid. The pine trees have never seen such a pretty goat. She is received like a princess. The chestnut trees lower their branches to the ground to stroke her. The flowers perfume the air. It is like a party. The little white goat has a lovely time, skipping about and eating things. She catches sight of Monsieur Seguin's little house in the valley, and laughs until she cries. She feels on top of the world. She falls in with a herd of chamois. One of them, we are told, even makes love to her. The old goat.

Suddenly, the wind freshens. The mountain turns violet. It is the evening. Already? Blanquette is amazed. Monsieur Seguin's house disappears in the mist. The herd of chamois tells her to go home, and they disappear. But she thinks about all the things that she will miss if she returns to the locked stable. She decides to stay where she is. Then she hears a rustling of leaves behind her. It is the wolf.

Enormous and immobile, the wolf is looking at the little white goat and tasting her in anticipation. Knowing that he will get to eat her, he is in no hurry. But whenever she turns round, he gives a wicked laugh. 'Ha, ha, the little goat of Monsieur Seguin!' and he licks his chops.

Blanquette feels lost. Remembering the story of old Renaude, who fought all night only to get eaten in the morning, she feels like giving up immediately. But the brave little goat puts up a good fight, forcing the wolf back ten times with her horns. Each time he retreats, she eats a little grass, then readies herself for the next assault. This lasts all night. From time to time she looks at the stars dancing in the sky and thinks, 'If I could only last until dawn...'

One after another, the stars go out. Blanquette fights on with her horns, the wolf with his teeth. A pale light appears on the horizon. The harsh cry of a cock comes from a small farm.

'At last,' says the little goat, who does not wait any longer to die. She stretches out on the ground in her beautiful white fur coat, all covered in blood. The wolf jumps on the little goat and eats her.

Goodbye Gringoire! And listen well!

Maybe Gringoire did listen well, for there is no mention of him that I can find in any dictionary or library. Perhaps he gave up lyric poetry and became a bank clerk. Unless he persevered with his ambition to be a poet, and his creditors got to him.

Daudet at least managed to keep the wolf from the door. He wrote a string of successful plays and novels, becoming rich in the process. But he succumbed to another occupational hazard of being a successful writer: venereal disease. His notes on his suffering, called *La*

Doulou, which have been translated by Julian Barnes under the title *In the Land of Pain*, make uncomfortable reading.

Daudet caught syphilis aged 17, apparently from a literary source. He told the writer De Goncourt that he had been seduced by a *lectrice de la cour*, a woman employed by the court to read out loud. After the initial infection and treatment with mercury, the illness lay dormant. He worked, married, and sired three children. But in his spare time he boasted that he was a 'real villain' with women, often sleeping with his friend's mistresses, and anyone else who was available. The syphilis came back, attacking his spinal cord. In 1885 the greatest neurologist of his time, J-M Charcot, said that Daudet was incurable. He lived on for another 12 years, trying mud baths and injections, even once hanging from the ceiling, suspended by the jaw. It did him no good.

He writes of his time in Lamalou at the Hotel Mas, just half an hour's drive up the road from us. The hotel has just reopened after refurbishment. It has been painted a rather nasty pink, enough to send many a designer screaming with pain into an early grave. There is also a theatre and a casino. It remains somewhere people come to be cured of incurable diseases, often dying in the process. The phrase 'going to Lamalou' is still used colloquially in the region to signify that people are ill. The French military send their wounded soldiers here to recuperate. It is often disconcerting to turn a corner of the street and see a battalion of wheelchairs descending down the hill, filled with out-of-control amputees.

By all accounts it was once an even more ghoulish place. Daudet's son Léon tells the story of an incident in the baths. A paralytic asks his neighbour: 'Excuse me sir, but is this leg yours or mine?'

'Yours I believe.' At which the paralytic falls over backwards and dies.

Daudet, bent almost double in pain, managed to keep a keen eye on his fellow sufferers. 'The Russian who can't move his arms and has a servant to roll cigarettes for him. They have a row; the servant has to make furious gestures for both of them.' Daudet used to visit the hot baths with his copy of Montaigne, stained with traces of iron and sulphur. The routine gradually got to him: 'Coming back again and again to the same place, like the wall you stood against as a child and on which they marked your height. A quantifiable change every time. But whereas the marks on the wall always demonstrated growth, now there is only regression and diminution.'

Daudet was never a tall man, but his suffering made him smaller. He is still remembered in Lamalou today, with a road named after him. He died on December 16, 1897. His son Léon also became a well-known journalist and writer, and married and divorced the granddaughter of Victor Hugo.

It is not recorded if Daudet ever went to Sète. Its cliff-top cemetery is a fabulous affair, a fine place from which to view eternity. Some of the tombs are large, almost like beach huts. We knew that Paul Valéry, France's most celebrated poet of the 20th century, was buried here somewhere, so we split up to try and find it. Here rest the families of sailors and local businessmen. Photographs sit on the tombs, as well as old flowers and yellow wreaths made of pottery, which look like deck quoits or giant bagels. On one grave stands a terracotta Madonna and child. The child's legs are broken and one of the mother's feet is chipped, but it is a lovely work. The Madonna carries a star on a stick in her hand, with the eye of God in the star. It was hot work looking for Valéry's resting place, but we found it eventually to the left of the entrance. It is a simple tomb, also commemorating the Grassis, his mother's family. On the tomb is written:

O récompense après une pensée
Qu'un long regard sur le calme des Dieux.

Valéry was born in Sète in 1871 and spent his childhood there. His father was a Corsican customs officer, while his mother was the daughter of the Italian consul to the city. When he was 13, they moved to Montpellier, but he spent his summers in Genoa, thus retaining his links with seaside towns. His first idea was to follow a career at sea, but his mathematics was not considered good enough. Instead he turned to literature, taking long walks along the seashore, composing poetry in his head and worshipping the work of Edgar Allan Poe, whom he called 'perhaps the subtlest artist of this century'. He fell in with a group of writers that included André Gide and Stéphane Mallarmé, then two of France's most celebrated writers. Perhaps paralysed by the shadow that Arthur Rimbaud threw over French poetry (anybody who abandons writing at the age of 17 must either be mad or a genius), Valéry did not publish anything until he was 40. His biographers say that his writer's block started during a night in Genoa where he apparently suffered a confidence crisis. His conclusion seemed to be that an artist's creation can never be perfect, because the product will always be inferior to what the artist first had in his mind. Better not to write, than to write something lesser than first intended.

He moved to London where he worked for three years as a clerk in Cecil Rhodes's Chartered Company. As a career, this sounds about as thrilling as T.S. Eliot's time working in trade finance at Lloyd's Bank. Valéry moved back to Paris, and married Jeannie Gobillard, the niece of the painter Berthe Morisot. He became private secretary to Edouard Lebey, who was the director of the Havas Agency, one of the first news agencies. His duties appear to have been refreshingly light, consisting of little more than reading the newspapers aloud to his boss. Valéry took to getting up at first light and writing a journal and poetry. Still nothing appeared in print until André Gide persuaded him to look again at his early poems with a view to publication in the *Nouvelle Revue Française*.

Valéry's first book was an instant success. His work is just the sort of thing that French intellectuals love. Dense, elliptic, virtually incomprehensible. In five years from 1917 to 1922 he published most of the poems that made him one of France's most important contemporary poets. By now he was a grey-haired man with a gaunt, ascetic expression. But his wit made him popular in society and he enjoyed the company of women. One of his most famous poems, *Le Cimetière Marin*, describes the view from the churchyard at Sète looking over the still sea:

> This quiet roof, where dove-sails saunter by
> Between the pines, the tombs, throbs visibly.
> Impartial noon patterns the sea in flame –
> That sea for ever starting and re-starting.
> When thought has had its hour, oh! How rewarding
> Are the long vistas of celestial calm.

The translation is by Cecil Day Lewis, poet laureate and father of actor Daniel Day Lewis. The 'quiet roof' is the sky; I have no idea what 'dove-sails' are, presumably some kind of bird, although sauntering is not what you expect from a dove, or perhaps they are boats. It's no more precise in French, which gives you an idea of what kind of writer Valéry is. The last two lines are a translation of what is written in French on his gravestone.

The only problem is that if you write a poem about a graveyard you are almost bound to end up in it. Valéry died in 1945, having seen out the war, but failed to last long once peace had been declared. He is remembered outside France for saying that an artist never really finishes his work, he just abandons it.

Sète's other famous son is the singer and songwriter Georges Brassens, who died in 1981. One of his best songs is *Supplique pour être enterré à la plage de Sète* – a request to be buried on the beach of Sète. His wish was not honoured. He was not buried in the hot sands, to be walked on by generations of young girls in small bikinis, but interred in the same cemetery. We didn't go looking for him. It was too hot and nearly lunchtime.

We had lunch with an Englishman who had known Lawrence Durrell when he lived in the Languedoc. Durrell had asked him one morning: 'What do you drink between brandy for breakfast and wine for lunch?'

Lawrence Durrell was one of those writers who made a career out of criticising English society, while living out of harm's way in the sunshine. He was born in Darjeeling, India and lived there for ten years until the death of his father. The family returned to England, but did not enjoy it. His Irish mother, when applying for a passport, claimed that she was Indian. Durrell wrote: 'English life is really like an autopsy. It is so, so dreary.' In later life he would claim that he had a Tibetan mentality – whatever that might mean. The story of how the family escaped to

Corfu in the 1930s was told by his younger brother Gerald in *My Family and Other Animals*. Lawrence went on to live in Greece, in Egypt, and in Yugoslavia, working as a teacher and a diplomat. While in Greece he wrote *The Black Book*, in which the hero, Lawrence Lucifer, struggles to escape the spiritual sterility of dying England, but finds in Greece warmth and fecundity. He had fallen under the spell of Sigmund Freud. Worse was to befall him. He wrote a fan letter to Henry Miller, who had escaped America and moved to Paris, where he began living and writing his series of books such as *Tropic of Cancer, Tropic of Capricorn* and later *Sexus, Plexus* and *Nexus*. These are fine books for adolescents, but as I grow older, I find them slightly ridiculous. Durrell and Miller became lifelong friends, writing long letters to each other and influencing each other's work.

The books that made Durrell's reputation were written here in Sommières. They make up the *Alexandria Quartet*, and consist of *Justine, Balthazar, Mountolive* and *Clea*. Durrell's prose is as lush as Liberace's bedroom. The exoticism is phoney, the characters stereotypical – but the French in particular love the books.

Durrell also seemed to love his new home. One of the attractions undoubtedly was the cheap wine, which he drank by the barrel, obviously not sharing Elizabeth David's opinion of the local brew. Durrell's last book, published in 1990, the year of his death, was called *Caesar's Vast Ghost*. Not surprisingly, it was reprinted in

America under the title *Provence*, with a comment on the cover from Erica de Jong. 'This is the sort of book I would love to have written,' she gushes. God knows why. It is a terrible book, written by the mind of an adolescent in the body of a man in his 70s.

Take a sentence from the introduction: 'Swerving down those long dusty roads among the olive groves, down the shivering galleries of green leaf I came, diving from penumbra to penumbra of shadow, feeling that icy contrast of sunblaze and darkness under the ruffling planes, plunging like a river trout in rapids from one pool of shadows to the next, the shadows almost icy in comparison with the outer sunshine and hard metalled blue sky.' Read quickly, this seems fine. But look a little closer. What exactly does it mean to dive from penumbra to penumbra of shadow? A penumbra already is a shadow. Do plane trees ruffle? What is sunblaze? It sounds rather Homeric, but is it a word? 'Plunging like a river trout' sounds good, but do trout plunge? In my experience, they just lurk in the depths. What is 'outer sunshine'? It all sounds plausible, but ultimately it is meaningless.

Later in the introduction he gives away what Provence meant to him – 'a calamitous intake of scarlet Fitou (douze degrés) or – wilier but no less hazardous for the hand with the pruning hook – red Corbières'. Now I don't want to come over all puritanical – I have been known to drink a glass of wine at dinner, although I prefer a Pic St Loup to a Fitou – but devotion to drinking should not mean abandoning the principles of writing a good, clear sentence.

A man who knew better than most people how to write a good clear sentence also spent some time in the Languedoc, although by the time he wrote *The Garden of Eden*, Ernest Hemingway had also undergone his own lengthy spell of devotion to the bottle. The writing at least is clear in *The Garden of Eden*, even if the thinking is a little muddled. The action begins in the crusader town of Aigues Mortes, another place that straddles Provence and the Languedoc. In fact both tourist boards claim it as their own and include it in their promotional material. The hero, David Bourne, is an American writer. His wife Catherine comes from a rich family. He has just written a second novel that is selling well in the States. She is jealous of his talent and success, but rich enough not to care if she ruins him. At first everything goes swimmingly. Hemingway describes the food beautifully, as well as the joy of being young and healthy and in love. Some people think they are not husband and wife at all, but brother and sister, a fact that excites the girl. They spend the mornings making love, eating breakfast, fishing, and planning lunch. The days are modelled partly on his own second honeymoon in the Camargue in 1927 with Pauline, for whom he had left his first wife. Then the mood takes a turn for the worst. Hemingway himself said that the theme was 'the happiness of the Garden that a man must lose'. Catherine begins to hint that she is about to do something 'wicked'. To begin with, this consists of having her hair cut short like an Eton schoolboy and acquiring as dark a tan as possible. Then she starts to act out a fantasy that she is in fact 'Peter', while he is 'Catherine'. Then she cuts her hair again, makes him dye his blond to match hers, and comes home with a dark-haired girl called Marita, whom she sleeps with. In time though, David starts sleeping with Marita, and Catherine starts going mad. Then she burns his writing and runs away.

Hemingway began writing the book in 1946 and kept at it for more than 15 years until his death. He complained to his editor, the legendary Maxwell Perkins, who had also been Scott Fitzgerald's editor, that 'he'd had a hell of a time' getting started and had been forced to 'go back and write much of it new where I did not have it right'. He never got it right, or at least was never happy enough with it to send it off to the printers. After the success of *The Old Man and the Sea* he had another stab at it, predicting at one point that it would be finished in three weeks. (You can understand why he didn't finish it. He had just been awarded the Nobel Prize for Literature. How keen would you be after that to finish a novel that has given you trouble for 15 years, particularly when you'd rather be fishing?)

When Hemingway shot himself with his double-barrelled Boss shotgun in 1961, the book was still sitting in galley proofs, bound in rubber bands. His estate gave the manuscript – some 1,500 pages – to a young editor at Charles Scribner's Sons offices in 1986. He cut it dramatically, getting rid of a subplot that involved a couple of characters called Nick and Barbara Sheldon. The tales of androgyny and a ménage à trois shed a different light on Hemingway, who emerges as a more complex character than a huntin' shootin' fisherman. This quote from *The Garden of Eden* also shows the innocence of the Camargue, when it was not a tourist destination: 'In those years only a very few people had ever come to the Mediterranean in the summer time and no one came to Le Grau du Roi except a few people from Nîmes. There was no casino and no entertainment and except in the hottest months when people came to swim there was no one at the hotel.'

When Hemingway picked up his Nobel Prize for literature he was too ill to travel in person to pick up the cheque, but he wrote a speech of acceptance. In it he mentioned three people who deserved the prize more, or at least as much as he did: Carl Sandburg, Bernard Berenson and 'that beautiful writer Karen Blixen'. Blixen is a Danish-born author, most famous for *Out of Africa* and *Seven Gothic Tales*. She spent the 1920s running a coffee plantation in Kenya while her husband, Bror, hunted lion and women. The farm failed. She was forced to sell up and return to the family home in Rungstedlund in Denmark to write *Out of Africa*, a romantic but unsentimental account of her love affair with Kenya.

One of the most surprising of her books is set in the Languedoc. She wrote *The Angelic Avengers* during the Second World War. It was published under a pseudonym, Pierre Andrézel. She called it her 'illegitimate child'. It is not hard to see why. It is the story of two beautiful girls, Lucan and Zosine, who, through a series of mishaps, end up as virtual orphans. The 1840s were a bad time to be single women without any money. They end up in the hands of Reverend Penhallow and his wife, who take them to live on their farm in the south of France. It turns out to be in the Languedoc:

'Six miles from the small town of Lunel, and about a mile and a half from the village of Peyriac, in a garden surrounded by a low stone wall, there stood a long, pink house. It was called "Sainte Barbe", and it had once been the main building of a farm.' Blixen seems to have a smattering of knowledge of the region: 'In the whole district of Peyriac, where the famous dessert wine Muscat de Lunel is grown, the vintaging is the great event of the year.' And: 'The cold north wind that people of the province called the mistral blew across the empty, faded vineyards.'

But did she ever visit the Languedoc? There is no mention of it in her biography. One suspects not. The landscape in the book is convincing enough, but the long, pink house must surely be a figment of her imagination. There are no old pink houses in the Languedoc, at least none that I have ever seen. The Languedoc for her is a dark, tumultuous place, where family histories remain forever mysterious, a place of the mind. The ascetic cleric turns out to be a white slaver, who, along with his wife, sells white women. He tries to do them in, but they escape, he kills himself, Zosine's father, who had fled his creditors earlier in the book, returns richer than ever, and the two girls marry handsome noblemen.

Generally I share Ernest Hemingway's opinion of Blixen's writing, although the suspicion remains that he spoke highly of her out of affection for her estranged husband, Bror, with whom he went hunting. At their best, her tales are fantastic and exotic. *Out of Africa* is written with an elegant restraint, almost as if by a female Hemingway, with short sentences and noble sentiments. *The Angelic Avengers* is almost by another hand altogether: soft and sentimental, with little humour. But I like the fact that it is set in the Languedoc.

Another person keen on pseudonyms was Patrick O'Brian, who moved after the Second World War to the little fishing village of Collioure, close to the Spanish border. He is the author of the Aubrey Martin novels, which are set at sea during the time of the Napoleonic wars. The detail is authentic. You feel, whether on land or at sea, that you are in the hands of a master storyteller, who understood the 18th century as well as Jane Austen. I used to take his books on long flights to Africa, but after two or three, I began to realise that I knew more about ships and men at war than I ever needed, so I stopped reading them.

However, it turns out that Patrick O'Brian did not exist. The author's real name was Richard Patrick Russ. He grew up in Buckinghamshire, not Ireland, and was of German descent. He came to live in Collioure in 1949 with his second wife, Mary Tolstoy. She was already the mother of Nicholas Tolstoy, the historian who was successfully sued for libel and bankrupted in the 1980s. He left behind a wife from a previous marriage, and a son. The couple also had a daughter, Jane, who had spina bifida and died aged three. Cut off in Collioure, O'Brian found the going hard. He worked as a translator and began turning out his naval novels, of which there are more than 20. He also wrote a biography of Picasso. It is an interesting work, full of colour and life and good on Barcelona and Picasso's time there. But you cannot help wondering how much you can trust a biographer who was at the very least economical with the truth about his own life. For O'Brian never came clean on his background. It took a snooping journalist to uncover the truth about his past. He had taken to wintering in Ireland and revelling in his late fame. His exposure came as something of a shock, given the air of veracity he brought to the naval series.

I went down to Collioure to look for traces of him. It is a small, pretty fishing village that used to be renowned for its anchovies. There are still two anchovy firms there, Desclaux and Roque. Guy Roque's grandfather started the business in 1870. But the work of filleting anchovies is tedious and time consuming. Most of it now takes place in places where labour is cheaper, such as Morocco. In O'Brian's time the U-shaped harbour would have been full of fishing boats – barques catalanes – until 1968, when they were accused of interfering with the tourists who came to swim, and banned from the beaches. They are distinctive, with a dhow-style sail. Henri Matisse and Fauvist painters came to paint in the 1920s. He did a couple of well-known paintings of the boats on the shore. The best bar in town, the Templiers, contains many paintings done at that time, many of them of the boats and the harbour, often swapped by the painters for drinks from the bar. The other striking thing in Collioure is the church spire that looks like a phallus. Salvador Dali, who grew up just along the coast at Cadaques, called it the 'Catalan cock'. Of Patrick O'Brian, there is very little trace. He has disappeared nearly as cleanly as Richard Patrick Russ.

The rain has eased a little now. I am sure there will be more writers coming out to the Languedoc. Everyone we meet seems to be writing a book on the area. The area is awash with media folk who can neither afford nor endure Provence. Soon you won't be able to move for books called *Lunch in The Languedoc* or *Me, An Olive Tree and a Glass of Wine*. The locals would love the kind of exposure these books would give them, but not the recent immigrants from Britain, who fear their rural idylls will be ruined. The other day a woman in a restaurant said to me that she hoped I wasn't going to do a Peter Mayle.

'If you mean by that write a lot of books, appear on television and make a fortune, then I'm sorry. I would be delighted to do a Peter Mayle,' I replied.

'I haven't read the books myself,' she continued. 'But I am told by people that they ruined the place. We wouldn't want that happening here. And he was so rude to the locals.'

'How do you know that if you didn't read the books?'

French people on the other hand seem positively amused by *A Year in Provence* and its sequels. They like to laugh at the people of the south, but then there has always been animosity between the north and the south. Northerners think the people of the south are idle, dissipated and uneducated. The people of the south don't care what they think.

Perhaps the book to write is one that purports to be by a Frenchman who moves to the middle of Sussex, Mayfield maybe, and relates his hilarious adventures there. He would write of the joys of the local pub, the extraordinary amount of drinking that goes on and how people vomit happily in the street, the problems in finding a plumber, the joy of the local food, which is mainly curry, rising house prices and the convenience of the local supermarket that is open 24 hours a day.

I guess wherever you live there is always a fear that one's peace and quiet will be ruined. The people of Sussex would complain if the village became overrun with foreigners. But we are all invaders. It is just a question of when we came. It is like that feeling when you get on a train and you have the carriage to yourself. You can open the window, stretch out on the seats and put your baggage anywhere. But then you pull into a station and newcomers get on. They want the window shut, your feet off the seat, and room for their suitcases. You sit in silence and fume. No doubt they will soon pull a hamburger from their pocket and start to eat it.

I did a story the other day on British people living in Normandy. I spoke to one couple who had been there for two years, living in a nice house, but miles from anywhere. It was like they were living in the middle of a cabbage.

'We love it here. But please don't tell anyone about it,' they said. Don't tell anyone about Normandy? How stupid is that? I wanted to tell them: I think you'll find that the English know about Normandy, ever since that guy William the Conqueror came over and won a big battle nearly a thousand years ago in Hastings. Instead I agreed to preserve their anonymity.

The Languedoc has been invaded many times in its history. I think this invasion of foreigners will last no longer than the Romans, the Visigoths, or the Arabs, and leave even less trace. Perhaps house prices will rise to such an extent that people will find Yugoslavia cheaper, or the new airlines will be banned by Brussels, or the euro will become so strong that nobody can afford to live in Europe. I remember when I was young in the 1970s being told that oil was about to run out and that cars would all run on water. Now we are being told that water is about to run out, and we shall all die of thirst. I feel confident that scientists will discover stores of water somewhere, perhaps in the Arctic, or perfect a way to turn salt water into drinking water. Either way, market forces, and in France, government forces, have a way of correcting what seems like an inevitable upward curve.

The rain is still streaking down the window panes, but if I time it right I can dash to the letter box, post this letter, get to the car, and still make it home for dinner. Good-bye.

La Croisade, Canal du Midi, Easter 2001

Stuck behind a woman in the butcher's –
a road, followed by a canal – spending the salt
tax – the Roi Soleil – a giant crop circle, made by
spacemen – the source in the Black Mountains –
murders in Roussillon common as bread
and wine – hungry, looking for a restaurant

*Y*OU ASK IF I could ever return to England. As an expatriate, I think you go through various stages. First, the euphoria of escape. Everything in the new land seems splendid. What might drive you mad at home, such as delays in shops while a little old lady spends 20 minutes choosing the exact cut of beef, is positively enchanting here. I passed through that phase about six months ago. I now find it infuriating, along with the fact that the shops all shut at 12 o'clock and don't open again until 3 o'clock or even later. 'Get on with it, you silly old bag!' I long to shout, as she rejects first this piece of beef, then that. Instead, I smile in that charming, self-deprecating way that the English have. Meanwhile, another old lady pushes in my way, and the process is repeated. This first stage of expatriate living includes shunning the company of any other people who speak English, while desperately trying to make friends with the locals. At the second stage, where I think I am now, you realise that you are never going to be French. Even when you try to talk to people in French, they answer in English. So far we have encountered only friendship, but we are known at the bakery as 'Les Anglais de Sainte Cécile' and I guess that won't change if we live here for 30 years. Does it matter? I don't know yet. Nor do I know what the third stage is, although I suspect that it means that you can never return to live in England again.

Here we have been doing something so leisurely, so slow, that it seems almost surreal. We are on a canal boat. The water sits as still as the water in a bath. On board this boat, it is so calm and tranquil that you could almost be on a lilo in a swimming pool. But how did somebody get so much water to stay in place, here in a land where moisture is sucked from the ground like orange juice through a toddler's straw? Sitting on this boat that does not rock, in the shade of the fabulous plane trees that grow on the banks of the canal, it is hard not to reflect on all the effort that went into construction of a water link between the Atlantic and the Mediterranean.

On this plain that runs between the sea and the hills, man has been moving for thousands of years. This is the route of the Via Domitia, the oldest Roman road in France, the road that the Romans built to link Narbonne, their first colony, with their capital in Italy. It runs through Provence to the Rhône, crosses the mighty river, then continues through Nîmes, Béziers, Narbonne and Perpignan, where it reaches Spain via the Panissar Pass. In fact the Romans went first to Spain, then headed north to Narbonne and beyond. Then they had the bright idea of linking Spain to Rome via a road. It is said to follow an even more ancient road, the road of Heracles, one that the hero trod when he travelled to Spain and the garden of the Hesperides. No matter. By the time the Romans took it, it would have been overgrown.

The Roman road hugs the coast. At no stage does the Via Domitia wander more than 20 kilometres from the sea. This is because the hills of the Languedoc act as a barrier to venturing further inland. After 30 kilometres the land begins to rise, as if to give people a better view of the sea. Within 50 kilometres there are high hills that give an entirely different climate. It is no longer Mediterranean. Olive trees do not grow there. The rainfall is greater. The air is cooler. But the coastal strip, while occasionally lacking in character, is ideal for roadbuilding, with no hills to traverse. However, there are large rivers to cross.

The builder of the Via Domitia was not the Emperor Domitian, who came a few hundred years later and was more keen on abolishing buggery than encouraging construction work, but an energetic consul called Gnaeus Domitius Ahenobarbus. In 118 BC he crossed the Rhône with his legions. His mission was to build a road to give year-long communication lines between Rome and Spain and allow Roman armies to march swiftly from one place to another. Apart from his road, which he did not live to complete, little is known about him. He fought a couple of fierce battles against two French tribes, the Allobroges and the Arvernes. His censorship – a position not unlike the Chief Justice in America, with the power to control public morals and the leasing of buildings and public areas – was marked by his severity of rule. The position was an old and important one, the power of which was gradually weakened by the emperors. Ironically it was his namesake, the emperor Domitian, who finally did away with the position by appointing himself censor for life.

Just as the coming of the railroad in America brought new towns to life, so did the Via Domitia boost trade between Narbonne, Béziers and Nîmes. For some reason Montpellier was bypassed, thus missing out on a thousand years of history. Narbonne, or Narbo Martius in Latin, was founded in 118 BC, possibly to guard the road, although it seems absurd for a city to guard a long road. It is more likely to have become a colony to produce food such as grain and wheat, as well as becoming a trading centre. Spanish products, such as metalwork, wine and pottery, were sent to Rome. Heavy goods were sent by ship. The rest were sent overland in carts, drawn by horses or oxen. At Ambrussum, a stopover on the route from Nîmes to Béziers, there remains a 20-metre stretch of the road. It is interesting to walk over the paved road, rutted with deep grooves, caused by cartwheels over the centuries. According to Strabo:

'This road is excellent during the summer, but in the winter and spring it is a quagmire, flooded by the rivers that can only be crossed by ferries or wooden bridges.'

Strabo may be right, but there is a stone Roman bridge near Saint Thibéry where the centurions and their impedimenta would have crossed the Hérault. There are still three arches crossing the river, each standing on a triangular base. Because an arch is stronger if the stones at the top are wider, the construction is tapered, each stone hand cut, with the smaller ones at the base and the larger ones in the centre. So solid and yet so graceful is the structure that it seems unlikely that the rest of the bridge was washed away. More probable is that some invading army at some point decided to cut down the options of any resistance crossing the Hérault. Near to the bridge is a 12th-century mill called Le Concasseur. It is a fine building, with tall towers and high arches to let the water flood through during the winter. Behind the mill is a new building, a hydro-electric dam, which silently goes about the business of producing electricity.

You can still see the outline of the Via Domitia from the hillside of the Oppidum d'Ensérune, but one's eye is also caught by a line of plane trees and the occasional passing boat on the water. Many people had dreamt of a canal to link the Atlantic Sea to the Mediterranean. Not only would it cut out a long and costly trip round the

Iberian peninsula, but it would create tolls and control for the King's treasury. It had been the dream of many Europeans, from Charlemagne onwards, to build the canal. You only need to look at a map of France to see how engaging the idea is of linking the river Garonne in the west near Bordeaux, which drains into the Atlantic, to the Aude, which drains into the Mediterranean to the east. But it took the technological developments of the Italians – Leonardo da Vinci is credited with inventing double swinging mitre lock gates, the type still predominantly used on canals to this day, when he acted as chief engineer to the Duke of Milan in 1482 – and the egotism and determination of two men: Louis XIV le Roi Soleil, and Pierre Paul Riquet, a native of the Languedoc who made a fortune as a salt tax collector.

Riquet was born on June 29 1604 in Béziers. He was educated at the Jesuit college where he showed early signs of pig-headedness by refusing to learn Greek, Latin or French, preferring the local tongue of Occitan. When he was 19, he married Catherine de Milhau, a local beauty with the added charm of a significant dowry, which enabled them to buy the château and estate at Bonrepos, near the village of Verfeil some 20 kilometres to the east of Toulouse. In 1630 he was appointed collector of the salt tax. It is argued that it is only the perifidious English in India and the French at home who have ever taxed such a basic commodity as salt. (Some suggest that the tax in France contributed to the French Revolution, but I prefer the theory that it was caused by the aristocracy's failure to play cricket with their staff – difficult I know, as the French have never played cricket. But the theory is that in England at least there was some social interaction between the landowners and their workers; in France there was nothing, only contempt on both sides.)

Roy Moxham has written an entertaining book called *The Great Hedge of India*, which describes in much detail the construction of a large thorn hedge in the 1850s to divide India from the Himalayas to Orissa. According to Moxham, it was planted by the East India Company to stop the smuggling of salt and other goods from one side of India to the other. The story is so implausible that I still can't decide whether or not the tale is an elaborate hoax. The Chinese, as usual, were ahead of the game, taxing salt as early as the 20th century BC. The first written mention of it is in a text called the Guanzi, written by an economics minister for the ruler of the state of Li, some time around 300 BC. Of course, with the introduction of the refrigerator and freezer, salt has lost its status, becoming almost a health hazard rather than a benefit, which makes Gandhi's salt march of the 1930s seem almost anachronistic.

Whatever the morals of the salt tax, it proved to be good business. Riquet raised so much money that he was put in charge of raising the tax for the whole province. Together with his brother-in-law, Paul Mas, he went into the arms business, supplying the king's army with provisions. It is not known when he first conceived his passion for building the canal. The idea had been mooted for more than a generation. Riquet's father, when serving as a local politician in Béziers in 1618, voted against a proposal to build a canal between the two seas. As L.T.C. Rolt observes in his rather dry account, *From Sea to Sea*:

'By now the projected canal between the two seas had been talked about and reported upon in the States of Languedoc without a single sod being turned.'

Such a lengthy delay will come as no surprise to anybody who has ever tried to get any building work done in the region. By the middle of the 1660s, this canal was becoming something of an obsession with Riquet. He spent many hours trying to solve the fundamental problem of how to get enough water for the canal. The canal was planned to carry sea-going vessels from sea to sea. It would need to be wide enough to accommodate them. In addition the hot climate of the Midi would evaporate a lot of water. I struggle sometimes to keep my swimming pool topped up with enough water in the summer months. Riquet was contemplating a body of water nearly 240 kilometres long, which would be two metres deep and 16 metres wide.

The most glamorous way to travel along the canal is on the Roi Soleil. This is a canal boat conceived and built by Guillaume de Pertuis and his wife Tracey, designed to pamper rich Americans. We first saw it going through the locks in Béziers. It is the longest boat on the canal, with a crew of six immaculately dressed in white. Thomas Jefferson travelled the length of the Canal du Midi in 1787. He put his carriage on the back of a barge and declared: 'Of all the methods of travelling I have ever tried, this is the pleasantest.'

He must have had the Roi Soleil in mind when he said that. For there is generally something a bit uncomfortable about canal boats. Compared to sailing, barging is like the difference between a coal train and the Orient Express. It has not been fashionable since Cleopatra swept up the Nile to seduce Mark Antony. It is a bit like caravanning on water.

But not on the Roi Soleil. It has linen sheets, showers you can fit into, and comfortable beds. 'Our inspiration is more yachting than barging,' says Guillaume. 'Her lines and mahogany and brass trim pay homage to the classic motor yachts of the 1920s.'

The Roi Soleil has two routes: one starting at Avignon, descending the Rhône until Arles, then joining the Rhône Canal until Sète, crossing the Etang de Thau with its celebrated oyster beds. The other route goes to the end of the Canal du Midi.

We joined them for a trip through the Camargue. As the boat surges up the narrow canal, herons and kingfishers follow in search of fish disturbed by the wake; horsemen round up the bulls in the evening sun, while in the distance the towers of Aigues Mortes are silhouetted against the sunset.

At first the pace seems very slow. But then you begin to appreciate the calm and the light. The canal is lined by plane trees, each trunk an abstract painting. Ducks gather near the bridges. Kingfishers wait on the trees. Joggers run past you; cyclists disappear round the bends. As a cure for stress it should be on the National Health.

To get a closer look at the Canal du Midi we went down to Colombiers, a pretty town just west of Béziers, where we had managed to get hold of a boat from Rives de France, a boat-hire company. It was a good-sized boat, the sort of thing that you would use to go fishing off the Florida Keys. But it was not very pretty. On the canal these boats are nicknamed 'Tupperware pirates' on account of their looks and the people who drive them. You can rent a boat to drive on the canal with just ten minutes' waterway experience. A man will take you out of the mooring, help you steer under a narrow bridge, and show you how to tie up to the bank. You are not allowed to tie up to the plane trees that line the canal, even though these seem tailor made for the purpose. Apparently joggers or cyclists might trip over the ropes and end up falling into the canal.

It was half-term, so we had a boatful. Hugo and Julia had flown out from England and were fighting in one of the cabins with their French friend Lulu; Olivia was up on deck, desperately trying to get hold of the wheel so that she could steer the boat into the bank; and an English friend, Simon, was there to help. Helena had very wisely decided to meet us down river. It was Bea's first birthday the next day, but she would only be allowed to come along for tea. Somehow the boatman decided that we were a reliable crew and allowed us to drop him off in the harbour. We stocked up with baguettes and pains au chocolat and headed out.

A canal trip is not ideal for those seeking speed and thrills. A walking pace is encouraged. The top speed allowed is eight kilometres an hour. Hugo steered for a little bit, but decided it was dull. He spent the day sitting on the deck, ostensibly in charge of spotting approaching vessels, but he turned out to be quite inadequate at this job. His lookout facilities only worked when he was prompted. We would spot an oncoming boat and call to him: 'Is there anything coming?'

'Yes,' he would reply, without looking up. Then he would go back to sleep. We motored on. It was a lovely autumn day, the plane trees' leaves coloured red and gold in the sun.

The canal wanders like a drunken sailor around Capestang. First you catch a view of Capestang from the east; then from the north; then suddenly Capestang can be seen in the east, the impressive tower of the church appearing like a will o' the wisp in every direction. The canal follows the topography of the land. Even though this meander is frustrating, it did not present too many technical problems for the builders. More taxing was the way through the hills near the Oppidum d'Ensérune, near the ill-fated tunnel of Malpas.

The Oppidum d'Ensérune sits on a small hill about a hundred metres above the vineyards, covered with pine trees and cypresses. Up here the air is fresh. High above us a buzzard wheeled in the wind. There are fantastic views in all directions: to Béziers and the cathedral of Saint Nazaire to the east; to the south and the hills of La Clape and the sea; the towers of Narbonne can be seen faintly to the west; while to the north stands the tower of Montady, the vineyards of Faugères and the mountains of the Cévennes looming blue in the distance. Directly below the hill to the north is a strange sight. It looks like a giant crop circle, made by spacemen, at least five kilometres across. In the 13th century it used to be a salt lagoon before the local monks began draining it in 1248. They dug long ditches towards one central point, where an underground reservoir takes the water to a sump in the middle. It took 20 years to dig the radial ditches, as well as an underground culvert that takes the water from the centre of the former lagoon to drain beneath the Ensérune ridge. It is amusing to imagine the monks up to their knees in mud, their cassocks hitched around their waists with the sun beating down on their tonsured heads. The drained ground proved to be very fertile. Each field is wedge shaped, with the different crops of vine and wheat producing a spectacular pattern on the ground, rather like the Palio square in Siena.

The town was inhabited from the middle of the 6th century before Christ – about the time that Homer was composing the Odyssey – until the 1st century after Christ, when the Pax Romana persuaded the inhabitants to forsake their hilltop for the easier living on the plain. From the hilltop, the inhabitants would have looked down on the lake and the surrounding countryside. They would have seen any hostile forces coming from miles away. As we stood looking at the view, we saw something equally grave. A coachload of German tourists was coming up the hill. We hurried to the entrance and walked inside. There is a small green fence that guides you around the site. You pass first along the northern edge, past houses built of pisé, which is a mixture of clay soil and pebbles and straw, then later stone. In the floor of all these houses is a large pot about the size of a fridge. This acted as a storeroom, where things could be kept cool in the summer.

There is a very southern Mediterranean feel to the place: you could be south of Rome on Capri, watching the swallows soar through the trees. The Graeco-Roman influence made itself felt on the architecture by about the 2nd century BC, with houses built around courtyards. Capitals and columns inspired by Ionic and Doric orders were erected, murals and mosaic floors put in place, while a sophisticated water system transported water from the spring to various cisterns around the town, with the sewage going in the opposite direction down the hill.

When the town was abandoned in the 1st century AD, it lay undisturbed for more than 2,000 years. It was a monk, abbot Ginieis, who first found traces of human occupation on the hill opposite his church in Montady, a small village west of Béziers. In 1915, when other Frenchmen were digging trenches in the north of the country to keep the Germans at bay, Félix Mouret, who had bought some of the land, began excavating the site. He built an elegant villa reminiscent of those on the Côte d'Azur, with large rooms, a columned entrance and a high tower giving even better views over the neighbourhood. This was Mouret's home during the course of his excavations, and was turned into a museum in 1937. Mouret also encouraged a splendid garden around the house, which stretches on past the car park to the east of the hill.

The museum was still empty of Germans when we went inside but full of Greek vases, small lamps that would have been fuelled by olive oil, and large pots. The workmanship is impressive. There is a large pot that stands by the door on the ground floor. You can trace with your thumb the mark that the potter made while it was still wet. There are also horse bits and fish hooks: two things that have not changed at all in the last 2,000 years. Presumably the inhabitants used the fish hooks in the lake that has now been drained.

After wandering around the museum we walked to the west of the site, where there is still some excavation work in progress. A couple of donkeys are grazing here, kept in the paddock by a thin rope. From up here, with the wind blowing fresh and cool and the swifts flying overhead, you wonder why anybody abandoned this spot for the heat of the plains.

It is a short drive down the hill to Nissan d'Ensérune, a small town that stands a few kilometres to the south. It has a good-looking church, a rococo style town hall, and a small square with a few shops and a couple of bars. The restaurant is typically French: at the bar a couple of men drinking, a pretty girl smoking, and a barman resting. There were four tables of diners, including some workmen spattered in paint. We sat outside in the shade of the plane trees and consumed a lunch that one could have ordered anywhere in France in living memory: a plate of charcuterie, a salad and cheese. The charcuterie was a tranche of pâté, some salami and some ham; the salad of tomatoes, lettuce and cucumber covered in dressing; and two cheeses, some Camembert and Roquefort, each individually wrapped. There was a jug of red wine and a carafe of water. Half way through lunch the street cleaner came up for a chat. He had been to England and wanted to talk about London. Then he swept up some leaves and went inside for a pastis.

Back on the boat we motored on. Julia and Lulu slept off lunch in their cabin, Hugo was busy killing flies, while Olivia sat on my knee and steered the boat. Simon had picked up a history of the canal, and was busy reading to us.

'Why was the tunnel called Malpas?' asked Hugo.

'Because a number of men were killed building it,' Simon explained. 'This hill threatened to put a halt to the entire project. The king was fed up with paying for the project and there seemed no way round the hill. But they managed to dig the tunnel in just nine days. Unfortunately, one of the main men was killed in the process.'

We passed through the tunnel. It is long and straight and wide. Parts of it are bricked, but there are sections at either end that have been left untouched, which have become pockmarked over the years.

'When the king's men came to break the news that work must stop, they travelled down in barges. They passed through the tunnel, lit by torches, then asked to see the hill that was causing all the problems, only to be told that they had just gone through it.'

The history of the canal began one autumn day. Pierre Paul Riquet put on his cape and hat, mounted his horse and trudged to the Black Mountains. His travelling companion was Pierre Campmas, the fontainier of Revel, who walked beside him carrying a large stick. A fontainier is a job title unique to France, which cannot easily be translated into English. Originally, no doubt, its derivation suggests that one of his roles was to ensure adequate supplies for the areas' fountains. He was also responsible for regulating and maintaining the water courses to minimise the danger of flooding. Campmas and his son, also called Pierre, knew the Black Mountains intimately. It is a wet, wooded country, full of streams and water courses. Here the three men wandered the hills, camped in the woods, and searched among the streams. Up on one of the peaks they found a watershed, which drained half to the west towards the Garonne and half to the east, to the Aude. For Riquet this was the equivalent of Archimedes' joyous discovery in the bath. Here would be the high point of the canal. Water could be sent both ways from here. This was where they decided to build a large dam, which would store water in the winter for release into the system during the dry summer months.

Back at his estate in Bonrepos, Riquet constructed a series of pilot dams and locks. His friend De Boulement was appointed Archbishop of Toulouse, making him the most powerful man in the Languedoc, investing him with all powers spiritual and temporal. He was invited to the estate to witness the working model and was so impressed that he suggested Riquet write to Colbert, the king's finance minister, together with a letter of recommendation from him. This letter, dated 26 November 1662, still exists. It is a masterly example of flattery, hyperbole and sycophantic drivel. Riquet appeals to the king's pride and power and tells him that this will make France rich while diminishing the power of the king of Spain. The letter was well received. The archbishop and Riquet were summoned to Paris to explain their plan in detail.

Louis XIV's men were right to be cautious. They were

planning the greatest civil engineering project since the time of the Romans. The sticking point – like all great projects – was how was it to be financed? Interestingly, the solution was a three-part package, consisting of money from the central exchequer; money from the Province of the Languedoc; and finally money raised in way of taxes by Riquet himself. In return, Riquet and his heirs would be granted control and the profits from any tolls, although the government would be allowed to set the level of the tolls (echoes of the 2001 energy crisis in California, caused by the state government's reluctance to allow private energy producers to put up their prices). The Canal du Midi was probably the world's first private and public financing partnership. It would reveal the flaws and benefits of any project financed in this manner.

Finally in 1666 Louis XIV issued an edict declaiming that work on the canal between the two seas would begin. It is a marvellous document, full of rhetoric and grandeur that you would expect from the world's most splendid and pompous ruler. Back in the Languedoc, work began. The first step was to build a reservoir and feeder system in the Black Mountains. The foundation stone of the St Ferreol dam was laid on April 15 1667. It was completed four years later. It was the most impressive civil engineering work of its time, possibly the major achievement of the whole canal project. It holds more than 180 million gallons of water. It was all dug and constructed by hand, much of it by women, who were paid a penny a load.

Equally impressive is the vision and attitude of Riquet. Even though the dam is in a remote valley in an obscure part of France, trees were planted, walks were made on the banks, and a giant fountain spurting some 60 feet in the air was placed at the foot of the weir. Carrying on the tradition of the great Renaissance engineers, who in turn were following the lead of the Romans with projects like the Pont du Gard, the civil works of the canal exude a sense of grandeur. It is a tradition of public works that still has not been lost in France, although it disappeared in Britain with the death of Isambard Kingdom Brunel.

Over the next few years, work continued on the canal itself, despite disputes with landowners and difficulties raising the taxes to pay for it. When Colbert, the French finance minister, questioned some of the tax-raising methods of Riquet's men, which was leading to revolt and virtual civil war, Riquet explained that this was the only method of dealing with the men of the Midi. 'Murders are as common in Roussillon as bread and wine,' he said. 'A neighbour kills his neighbour, and a brother his own brother. No human power could prevent this kind of men killing each other, and you may therefore infer that the tax collectors are subject to the same fate. In this country, the tax collectors are always on the lookout; they kill just as they are killed; it is the only way to carry out their function.'

Numerous technical problems needed to be overcome. A prize was offered to all the universities of Europe if they could come up with a solution for keeping the canal free of weed. Grandvoinet, the geographer royal, travelled to the canal and after careful consideration, came up with an answer. There is a water-colour drawing he made which is now in the archives of the canal offices. It shows in great detail how this weed would be kept at bay. Conveniently it is pictured growing like grass. A boat is pulling two rollers on chains, which are cutting a neat swathe through the floor of the canal like a mower on an English lawn. Unfortunately, this neat solution proved impractical. In the end, they had to rely on dredging and ducks to keep the weeds at bay.

Like all large engineering works, the biggest problem was financial. By 1675 the money was beginning to run out. Paris did not want to sink any more cash into a large trench in the Languedoc. So Riquet did something almost unthinkable. He instructed his solicitor to start selling his properties. Now aged seventy-three, Riquet was prepared to sell his daughters' dowries and pay for the work himself in order to complete the project. As he bitterly remarked: 'I have made a canal to drown myself and my family.'

He didn't even live long enough to drown himself in it. There was just one short section of the canal left to be dug, from the river Hérault to the Etang de Thau, the large inland body of salt water, separated from the Mediterranean by a small spit of land, when Riquet fell ill. He summoned his son to his bedside and asked how much more there was left to dig. One league he was told. 'One league,' repeated Riquet. They are reputed to be his last words. He died on October 1 1680, owing more than two million livres.

There is a statue of him in Béziers, near the bottom of the Allées Paul Riquet, the shaded ramblas in the centre of the city. It was erected in 1838 following a public subscription organised by the Archaeological Society. He is dressed almost like a pirate, with calf-length leather boots, a cape, puffed sleeves, a cravat and a thin moustache. He is supposed to be looking west towards his canal and the Atlantic Ocean, but in reality he is looking at the ground, as if weighed down by the pigeons that settle on his head.

His son and descendants were left to settle the bill for building the canal, but were then able to reap the benefits of their ancestor's work. It took a long time coming. The canal cost a total of 15,249,399 livres, exceeding the budget by more than 6,000,000 livres, like all the best earth-moving projects. This does not even include the money spent on building the new port of Sète, which was constructed to handle all the traffic between the canal and the Mediterranean.

'I'm hungry,' said Hugo. 'It's been a long day.' We stopped at Capestang for ice creams and looked at the church. It was market day and the busy square was full of people selling oysters, walnuts, cheese, vegetables, books, bread. There was an unhurried air to the place that I liked.

A number of old men stood around chatting to each other, as if they had been friends for generations. While the children ate their ice creams we lingered in a bar and had a cup of coffee.

Back at the boat, we manoeuvred our way through the narrowest bridge on the canal, and motored on. We were due to meet Helena and Bea at Le Sommail, some two hours down river. This stretch is one of the best on the canal. There are no locks, just thousands of plane trees, the occasional pedestrian and glimpses of fabulous houses hidden in the trees.

After an hour the children got restless so we threw them off the boat and had them run alongside. Finally we reached Le Sommail where the rest of the party was waiting for us.

Bea enjoyed a rather eccentric first birthday party, then we managed to get rid of the children for the evening. They went off with Lina the au pair, while we enjoyed a glass of wine.

My plan on the way down had been to motor back up the canal to a restaurant. I had kept a bit of an eye open and I recalled there had been the perfect spot just an hour upstream. A little auberge, perched by the side of the canal, overhung with wisteria. I envisaged a pot au feu, a good bottle of Languedoc red wine, some Reblochon cheese, black coffee, perhaps even a glass of brandy. We cast off from Le Sommail. It was already getting cool. The sun was low through the trees. We were followed most of the way by a heron, who was keen on watching our wake in case it stirred up any fish. The cyclists and walkers had disappeared. There were no more boats moving. A mist was beginning to fall. Walking pace is fine when you are not in a hurry. But when you have a hungry wife to feed, it seems painfully slow. I increased the revs on the engine. Helena went below and found the lights for the boat. It was like being a commando, sweeping up the canal in a dusk raid. The heron had disappeared now; too dark for fishing. But still there was no sign of our restaurant.

Finally we turned a corner and there it was, perfect in every way, except one. It was closed. Helena looked at me. I looked at the restaurant.

'I have heard that there is a better restaurant a bit further up stream,' I said.

'Better, as in, open and serving food?'

I ignored her and gunned the engine. This was the last weekend that the canal would be open. Soon the rainy season would begin. Hadn't I read that it rains more here than in Paris? I increased the revs some more. The boat began to move and throw up a wake that washed against the banks. Our walking pace had turned into a trot and swiftly a gallop. A long half hour passed slowly. Helena kept going down to the cabin and emerging in another layer of clothing. 'Are you sure there is another restaurant on the canal?' she asked, twice. There wasn't a light to be seen. I wasn't sure there was anybody left alive in the south of France, so dark was it. All we had on board was half an uneaten chocolate birthday cake and a bottle of Château Paul Mas wine.

Finally we came alongside the Auberge de la Croisade. We moored hurriedly, tying up to two plane trees and not bothering with the tent pegs. It was eight o'clock, pitch black. We stumbled along the towpath into the restaurant. It was enormous, with at least 20 tables laid for dinner. There was just one couple in the place, English, who were reading last week's *Daily Telegraph* without much enthusiasm.

'Table for two?' I said to the waitress.

'Have you booked?' she said.

'No.'

She went off and consulted the manager. Yes, she could squeeze us in. We sat down and laughed at our good fortune to get a table in an empty restaurant. Then the customers started arriving. And arriving. Within 20 minutes the place was packed. Within half an hour people were being turned away. We ate our pot au feu in stunned silence, drank the wine, decided against the brandy, and went back to the boat, where we listened to the leaves in the trees and the cars going by on the road in the distance before falling asleep.

Saint Siméon, September 2001

A choice of château – the Seigneurie de
Peyrat – a little yellow bug – vineyards walk
to the sea – land of red gold – wine riots
in Béziers – thin wine, without aroma
or taste – a day's grape picking

ONE WARM SUMMER'S AFTERNOON I was sitting in
the office of Baron Gilles de Latude, scion of one of
the oldest wine-growing families in the Languedoc. He
lives on a beautiful estate called Bourgade, halfway
between Pézenas and Béziers. With me is Jean-Claude
Mas, another wine maker with a large estate near Pézenas.
Unwittingly, I am a witness at a classic confrontation
between Old France and New France, between a declining
aristocracy and a rising mercantile class. Although there is
only ten years in age between the two men, the gap is
rather more than half a generation. Jean-Claude makes
more than three million bottles of wine a year, travels the
world to sell his product, speaks fluent English and plays
tennis on the rare occasions that he has a morning off.
Gilles speaks beautiful French but no English, would like

to make his own wine but knows that would be an enormous investment, which might fail to pay off, and besides, he would rather be out shooting.

Gilles is a handsome man with a high forehead, prominent nose and a penchant for striped shirts. The head of a deer looks down on him, along with an old-fashioned map of France, and portraits of his hunting dogs. Even the air in the office is cool and subdued, as if it has been around forever, or has been produced by an aristocratic filter. There are no computers, just an old telephone with a round dial and a couple of notebooks. An old dresser stands in the corner, in which lie the accounts of the farm for generations, all copied out in neat copperplate hand. The family has been a force in the area for more than 200 years. When Gilles' father was due to inherit, he was given the choice of three of the finest châteaux in the region: Belles Eaux, Fondouce or Bourgade. He chose Bourgade, partly because he lived there anyway, but also because he loved its proximity to the sea. He was a naval officer who enjoyed spending his spare time on the coast near Marseillan, where he kept a sailing boat.

The de Latudes made a fortune in the days when anybody with land was growing grapes and making wine, which was sold to thirsty miners or soldiers. The army of France marched on the cheap thin wines of the Languedoc. It was not the quality of the wine that made the growers so much money, but the quantity. On the plains of the Hérault, a hectare of vineyard could yield six times as much as the equivalent in Bordeaux or Burgundy. The de Latude family did not bother itself too much with commerce. They reaped the profits, but were reluctant to reinvest. And as so often happens with French families, there were frequent disputes over money.

When his father died, Gilles asked his brother what they should do about the inheritance, because in France this is normally split equally between all the children. His brother replied that he wanted nothing to do with the land, but he would take the château. Gilles took over the estate and farm buildings. The other estates, Fondouce and Belles Eaux, had both been sold, while parts of Bourgade have been turned into a golf course with the château divided in two by the family.

Sitting across from the desk in the large airy office is Jean-Claude Mas. Mas is a good-looking man with dark hair and an MBA from Birmingham University. He is an enthusiastic tennis player, fiercely competitive although with a rather erratic serve. His family came originally from Saint-Pons-de-Mauchiens, a pretty village on the left bank of the Hérault river. His grandfather managed to buy Château de Conas on the outskirts of Pézenas in the 1950s.

Nobody wanted a large château in those days. They were expensive to run and hard to heat. He bought it for a song. He was only really buying it for the vineyards that surrounded the property. The other château owners in the region rather resented this upstart and did not include the family in their shooting drives or drinks parties, not that he would have wanted or even had time to attend them. He was too busy trying to make a living from the vineyards.

After graduating from Birmingham University, Jean-Claude went to work in Miami for the French Development Authority, then he came back home to take up the family business. He knew that to be taken seriously, he needed to produce better wine. He had learnt from his time in America that people buy brands, not individual bottles. So he started developing attractive labels, heavy bottles and very drinkable wine. He concentrates on building up large export markets, sending his wines to America, Japan, and some of the best wine bars in London, such as the Match Bars, where they sell for around £25 a bottle.

Gilles de Latude sat back in his chair, looked across his desk and said: 'So what is it you want?'

Jean-Claude did not want anything. He was there at the request of Gilles' wife, Ruth, another formidable Yorkshire woman, who had left the north of England more than 20 years earlier to become an au pair in France. She fell in love with a Frenchman and married him. Three children later, after a number of happy years in Paris, she moved back to the Languedoc with him to his ancestral property, the Abbaye de Valmagne. It is one of the few monasteries that was saved after the revolution when it changed from saving souls to producing wine. One of the most incongruous sights in the Languedoc is the giant barrels of wine in the crypt of the church.

Eventually the marriage fell apart and she moved in with Gilles. When he had taken over the estate seven years earlier, he had begun growing grapes. It is said that God hates a primary producer. For if conditions are good and disease or floods are absent for a few years, competition grows, and prices fall. This has been the fate of wine prices in the Languedoc. After a tremendous boom in the 1990s, when wine critics fell over themselves to lavish praise on the growers of the region, the prices of bulk wine, particularly that made by the cooperatives, began to fall. In the two years between 1999 and 2001, the price for growers of Chardonnay grapes had almost halved. Robert Skalli, a pied noir, one of the immigrants from the Maghreb who made such an impact on this region since their arrival in the 1960s, had just telephoned Gilles de Latude with the news that he would need to reduce his prices by 10 per cent. They had declined by 10 per cent the year before.

Skalli was offering between two francs and two francs fifty for a kilo of grapes. For this, the grapes would have to have been grown and picked. A kilo of grapes makes a bottle of wine. Imagine this, next time you open a bottle of wine: the cost of the contents is around 25 pence. This does not include the cost of vinification, bottling, storage, marketing etc. Nevertheless, the cost of producing a bottle of wine – even a good one – should not be much more than £1. For the most labour-intensive estates, with hand-picking and much work in the vineyards, you can maybe double that amount.

However you looked at it, Gilles was being squeezed. Skalli's meagre offer would barely cover his costs. He pulled a large leather-bound notebook from a drawer and read the amounts that he was being offered. Merlot – 2.80 francs; Cabernet Sauvignon – 2.60 francs; Cabernet Franc – 2 francs; Syrah – 2.50 francs; Grenache – 2.60 francs. Perhaps Jean-Claude could pay a little bit more?

It reminded me vividly of the moment in your favourite book, *The Leopard*, when Don Fabrizio realises that his world is finished, torn apart by Garibaldi and his liberal followers. The Leopard's noble lineage, his prestige and certainly his money are being usurped by the mafia mayor Don Calogero. As Tancredi, the nephew of Don Fabrizio, so wisely pointed out: 'If we want things to stay as they are, things will have to change.'

Jean-Claude is not Don Calogero; in looks and manner, he is more like Tancredi. But this meeting was symbolic of so many that have taken place in the Languedoc over the last 20 years. The old ways are no longer acceptable. Even though Gilles de Latude makes the pretence of being in command of the meeting, it is he who has been forced to turn parts of his château into a gîte. Paying guests drink the only wine he produces, a rosé made by the local cooperative in Montblanc. He does not have the money to invest in a winery. He cannot afford to replant his vineyards. Jean-Claude, on the other hand, has two wineries and a bank manager begging him to borrow money. If Jean-Claude cannot come up with a better offer than Robert Skalli, de Latude will be forced to accept a pitiful amount for his grapes and his labour.

The de Latudes are one of three big families in the area. The others are the de Berthiers and the Viennets. Arnaud de Berthier has one of the largest estates in the Languedoc, where he produces a bewildering amount of different bottles, mainly for the export market. Luc Viennet and his English wife Beatrice live in the Seigneurie de Peyrat, just north of Pézenas. When Luc Viennet was 18, he lived in an apartment in the best part of Paris, along with his older brother, a cook and a chauffeur. It was 1968. It is no surprise that when the students started rioting, Luc did not go along himself, but sent his chauffeur to pull up paving stones.

After a spell with a French bank in London, and marriage to Beatrice, he returned to Pézenas and the family business. His father by all accounts had been quite entrepreneurial, buying bulk wines from Algeria and Sicily, and planting new varieties of grapes in the Languedoc. Luc worked for a time with his older brother, but they found it difficult to agree on certain aspects of the business. Eventually he ended up with the Seigneurie de Peyrat and 180 hectares of land.

A seigneurie is a large manor house. Luc's great

grandfather, Gustave Fayet, bought it in 1910, mainly because he was interested in the vineyards and the winery. He already owned a substantial number of houses in the region, including the Abbaye de Fontfroide, which he bought partly to stop it being carted off to the Rockefellers' medieval museum in New York. Peyrat was accustomed to benign neglect. It dates from the 16th century. When Luc and Beatrice moved in at the beginning of the 1980s, it had been uninhabited for 150 years. At least it had escaped the craze in the late 1800s, when many of the large houses were turned into mini versions of Versailles. The worst thing that happened to Peyrat was when it was owned by a family of Jansenists. They were against any sort of ostentation or ornament and knocked down the towers and plastered over the frescoes in the chapel. The ground floor of the house has now been restored. The rooms are huge, with four-and-a-half metre high ceilings. This is a place for entertainment on a grand scale. The gardens have been partly restored, and an avenue planted of olive trees, cypresses and lavender bushes.

Luc insists that he was one of the first to plant Viognier in the Languedoc. Beatrice recalls the day they had a lunch in the Rhône valley. Luc ordered a bottle of wine, tasted it, and said: 'This is the sort of wine I want to make.' They now produce more than a million different bottles of wine a year, much of which is sent to England.

Viognier seems to have a particular influence on some

people. Others find it too strong, too scented, too much like marzipan. But Madame Verena Wyss, like Luc Viennet, fell under its spell. She bought Domaine Cante Perdrix, in the countryside outside Gabian, at the end of the 1980s. She and her husband ran a successful interior decorations shop in Zurich, but on a trip to the region fell madly in love with the place. Initially they envisaged that it would be a second home, a holiday retreat. They found a local labourer, who agreed to tend the vines. They hired some builders to convert the house. But every time they visited, they found that the work had either not been done as scheduled, or had been done incorrectly. So they sold the shop in Zurich, and began to make wine.

Madame Wyss's winery is a cross between a Swiss chemical plant and an interior architect's shop. Everything is simple, but beautiful. There is a steel spiral staircase. The oak barrels are stored in a separate building, turned slightly on their side to stop evaporation. 'This is a trick I learned from visiting Cheval Blanc in Bordeaux, and talking to their winemakers,' she says.

Her wine is now a success. As well as the Viognier, she makes a Roussanne, another white grape from the Rhône valley and a red wine called La Tonga. It is a blend of Cabernet Sauvignon and Merlot, the classic claret blend. For my taste it needs a lot of ageing. The oldest bottle I have tasted, a 1998, could have done with a bit more time.

Wine has always been a difficult business. Everyone

agrees now that to succeed, you need to have a successful brand and to be in control of everything from growing the grapes to selling the bottles, just as Madame Wyss does. But to develop a brand is an expensive thing to do, and difficult. In the Languedoc, people were never really wine makers. They were really grape growers. They don't even seem that keen on drinking the stuff. It is surprising to notice in this land of wine production that nobody drinks wine in the bars. The men drink either beer or pastis, the aniseed-flavoured drink that comes from Marseille, although in other guises it can be found along the Mediterranean coast, as ouzo in Greece, for example, or raki in Turkey; the women don't seem to drink anything at all.

Wine is only drunk during mealtimes and then not in any great quantity. I saw a photograph in the *Midi Libre*, the local newspaper. A group of wine producers had blockaded the road in protest at falling wine prices. They were sitting on the pavement and sharing a drink. You might think they would be drinking wine, but no, they were halfway through a large bottle of Ricard 51.

The Languedoc's wine boom began in the 1800s. An Occitan poet recalled in a poem his shock at returning to his homeland after years of travel abroad only to find that the hills had been covered in vines. 'What are these sticks covering the land I love?' he laments. It was quickly discovered that wine grew well in this climate. Between 1840 and 1870 more than 200,000 hectares were planted.

The province's only problem was access to the markets. Burgundy had managed to create a monopoly on trade with Paris. Bordeaux managed to exploit its connection by sea to England and the Netherlands. It was to help with the transport of this liquid gold that Pierre Paul Riquet determined to create the Canal des Deux Mers. But just as trade was booming, disaster struck in the form of an immigrant from America.

Phylloxera is a small yellow aphid. Its ability to attack the roots of vines makes it the most potent enemy of wine growers in the history of its cultivation. It came by boat from the East Coast of America, where it is a native, some time in the 1860s. American vines had gradually built up a resistance, but the effect on French vines was catastrophic. Almost 2.5 million hectares of vineyard was destroyed by a little creature that cared nothing for the grand châteaux or humble smallholdings. Its entry into French soil may have come via the Languedoc. The first printed report of it in France was in a letter written by a vet in 1867 in which he refers to a troubled vineyard in St Martin de Crau, just 35 kilometres northeast of Montpellier. There were also reports circulating of infected vines in Narbonne and the Gard. Bordeaux did not suffer a serious outbreak until about 10 years later. A body called the Hérault Commission set out to investigate the matter. One of the committee members, Jules Planchon, was particularly well qualified. He had been trained at Kew Botanical Gardens. There he had noticed that infected oak trees had been ravaged by small yellow insects. He spotted similar yellow insects on the roots of infected vines and deduced that they were responsible for the devastation. Few were prepared to accept this as the source of the problem. Politicians and clergy preferred to lay the blame with the immorality of the population, or the weather, soil exhaustion or overproduction. Imagine the despair in watching your livelihood wither before your eyes.

By June 1873 the situation was so bad that a prize of 300,000 francs was offered for anyone who could come up with a solution. Like all such competitions, it produced its share of mad suggestions. Among the silliest was the advice to irrigate the vines with white wine, although there is some made in the region to this day that could be best put to this use. Another was to bury a live toad in every vineyard (presumably to eat the aphids). Entries poured in from all over the world, including Sweden and Singapore, countries not renowned for their expertise in wine making.

Planchon had noticed that vines which grew in sandy soils were unaffected by the bug. It was also thought that flooding the vines would prevent the roots becoming infected. Like Macbeth's marching wood to Dunsinane, the vineyards of the Languedoc moved south, from the hills to the coastal plain. In one swift act, the seeds of the Languedoc wine lake of the 1970s had been sown. Vines produce their best grapes on poor soil, when they have to struggle to produce grapes. Plantations on the hills, which produce a low yield but a high-quality grape, were abandoned. Some of them remain empty to this day, desolated hamlets with the roofs falling in and graveyards where no new bodies have joined the dead since the 1870s. Growers found that not only could they limit the spread of the aphid by flooding and sandy soils, but their yields were even greater. The wine was of low alcohol content and even lesser taste content, but the palates of the 1800s were perhaps less discerning than today.

Flooding was not the final solution for the yellow aphids, which turned out to be very tenacious. Not every vineyard in France could march to the coast. The solution to producing phylloxera-resistant vines became to graft French vines on to American rootstock. This was an enormous job, one that is still done to this day. You only have to look at a hillside of vines to appreciate how long it would take to complete. There was also opposition from growers and drinkers, who questioned whether this would have an effect on the quality of the wine. It is a sobering thought that all the wines one drinks in France today, from the noble Château Latour to the thin vin de pays is grown on American rootstock. Wine lovers in Burgundy restricted this practice until 1887, by which time wine makers were grafting under cover of darkness to save their vineyards. Despite numerous attempts by interested parties, the prize money was never handed over, but phylloxera was under control.

By the middle of the 1880s, with phylloxera beaten and the railways built, money flowed into the Languedoc on a scale that had never been seen before. The vineyards stayed in the plains, closer to the railway stations and the lucrative markets of the north. The vineyard owners made so much money that they were inspired to start a craze for building outlandish châteaux – there are nearly as many in the small area around Béziers as in the whole of Bordeaux – with a bewildering number of designs, ranging from Scottish-looking castles to elegant façades that would not look out of place on the Boulevard Haussmann. To drive around the neighbourhood of Béziers is to be surprised at every corner by yet another lurking monolith, hidden like an elephant behind enormous trees. Here there will be a classical design; next door a Gothic monstrosity; down the road a Tuscan-style villa with a tower commanding excellent views over the vineyards and idle pickers. Unfortunately many of these 'Castles in Spain' were built next to the road. Busy traffic now thunders past their elaborately carved gates.

Their turrets, towers, shuttered windows, wrought-iron gates and elaborate gardens contrast markedly with the buildings of previous generations, which were designed with defence in mind, or soberly so as not to invite attention or intruders. The ancient châteaux in the region are surrounded by small houses and shops built in a circulade for safety like the shells of a snail. In times of danger the inhabitants would hide in the château and attackers would have to destroy the houses to get at the château. Even many of the religious buildings incorporated some of the design features of a defensive castle.

What inspired this building boom? Was it just a moment of madness, a subconscious desire to show the rest of France that the south was once again a powerful place, capable of monumental acts, or was it just the vanity of the nouveau riche? Maybe it was a little of everything. The châteaux – and this is perhaps why so many were built close to the road, so they were visible – were certainly designed to be gaped at, to surprise the passerby with the quality and scale of the building. Each château builder seemed eager to outdo his neighbours with an even more outlandish design.

Take Château de Grézan as an example. It sits on the plain 15 kilometres north of Béziers near the village of Laurens. Seen from afar, it looks like a village itself. As you coast down the hill you notice a mass of turrets and thick stone walls, battleship grey, rising above the vines. Its large castellated walls echo those of Aigues Mortes, built down by the coast 700 years earlier. But the work at Aigues Mortes was paid for by the King's treasury. The walls at Grézan were financed by Gabriel Mirepoix's wine crop. He enlarged the existing house, built an enormous cellar and died unmarried in 1924. As you cross the barbican you expect to meet maidens with long hair, their breasts forced into tight bodices; knights in shining armour mounted on enormous Percheron horses; and minstrels playing on a lute. Instead, there is an empty restaurant, a shed full of tractors and a wine shop containing a few dusty bottles.

If Château de Grézan is a crusader castle under siege from vines and now from tourists, Château La Jourdane is a vast neo-classical design made of brick and stone, which would not look out of place in central Europe. Antoine de Cassagne de Saint-Jean de Libron was ennobled by Léopold II, prince of Austria, Hungary and Bohemia, and grand duke of Tuscany. His coat of arms is sculpted into the walls of the red brick building. It was built by his son Etienne between 1860 and 1869. The length of construction was governed by the fact that he did not want to spend more than 45,000 francs a year, so once that amount had been spent, work was finished for the year.

Few were as prudent as this nobleman. Many were new to landowning. They believed that this new-found prosperity would last forever, unaffected by aphids or Algerian growers. Many, like the de Latudes, had seized their chance after the revolution. Before that most of the large estates had been in the hands of the church. More than 80 top estates were transferred into private hands.

The interiors of these châteaux are every bit as grand as the exteriors, although decay, theft and negligence have played a part in their decline. Enormous staircases were built, marble halls, and wood-panelled rooms to which the finest musicians were invited to play. The composer and pianist Camille Saint-Saëns, then the greatest name in French music, was hired for a concert tour in Béziers. For a Parisian this must have seemed as remote as playing in an Amazonian opera house. However, the money must have been good, for Gabriel Fauré, Jules Massenet and Déodat de Séverac all made the long journey to play for the local bourgeoisie.

As well as building themselves incredible palaces, the owners lavished money on the source of their income, the wine cellars. Normally situated next door to the château, the wineries are like temples to Bacchus. With incredible wooden ceilings, like the hull of a boat or the interior of a Norman cathedral, often dimly lit and cool away from the glare of the midday sun, they contain enormous wooden barrels, capable of holding many hundreds of litres of wine.

The good times did not last. Cheap imports from Algeria began to threaten the prosperity of the region, as did the practice of making wine from sugar and raisins. Things came to a head in 1907. Overproduction led to a serious wine glut. Prices fell. There were riots throughout the region, in Béziers, Montpellier and Narbonne. On June 9 more than half a million people gathered in Montpellier, with their leaders saying that if something was not done to help the wine growers, they would not pay their taxes. When the government failed to act, town councils throughout the region resigned. On June 19, troops were used against demonstrators, resulting in one death and at least ten injuries. A law was passed on June 29 aimed at helping the wine growers, but the problems were not solved. In many respects the arguments continue to this day, exacerbated now by all the new wine-growing areas such as Australia, America and South Africa.

After the First World War the price of wine slumped and did not recover until the Second World War. The ornamental lakes dried up, the lawns were not cut or watered, the peacocks were eaten and the trees in the orangeries died. Some of the inheritors of the châteaux locked the shutters and moved into smaller houses in the towns, which were easier to heat and cheaper to run. Other estates were kept alive by maiden aunts who eked out a lonely existence in their empty turrets, or turned them into apartment blocks for immigrants from the Maghreb. It was left to a later generation to revive the properties, partly because they wanted the land that went with them.

The region's nadir was probably the 1970s. Subsidies were needed to pay for the production of tasteless wine that nobody wanted to drink. The French country habit of drinking a litre of thin red wine a day was beginning to decline. Yet again there were riots. A policy of pulling up vines was introduced. It continues to this day, because even though the area has attracted great wine makers, it is still producing too much wine.

Towards the end of August, small tractors pulling even smaller trailers appear on the roads. They are narrow in order to get up the rows between the vines, but to anybody accustomed to large grain trailers in Sussex, they look comical. It is only when you start to fill them with grapes, that you realise they are a decent size. Much of the picking is done mechanically, with tall machines rather like a forage harvester. They have a belt that runs through the plants, pulling the grapes from the vines. Strangely, they appear to do very little damage to the vines.

The best wines are still picked by hand. In an attempt to get a first-hand view of the action, I agreed in a moment of madness to help Peter Glynn Smith with his grape picking. He has a small two-hectare vineyard of Cabernet Sauvignon grapes. He sends his grapes to the Pézenas co-operative, but this year decided also to make a row or two for himself, with the help of Jean-Claude Mas.

Peter told me to arrive at his house at eight o'clock sharp one September morning. We stayed up late the night before, carousing by the pool, and did not have time for breakfast, not even a cup of coffee. When we got there the house was deserted. There was just the sound of somebody singing in a bathroom. I called Peter's name and heard his voice: 'They are all in the vineyard. Sadly I won't be able to join you because I have done my back in.' Then the singing resumed.

At the vineyard all was action. There were 12 of us in total, with one driving the tractor. You are given a pair of secateurs and a bucket. It is your job to fill the bucket with grapes. When you have filled the bucket with grapes, another bucket appears, and you have to fill that one. This went on for four hours without stopping. The best way to get at the grapes is on one's knees. Then you cut the stalks of the bunches, careful not to take off one of your fingers with the secateurs. The job is at once monotonous and uplifting. There is something satisfying about manual labour. The bunches of grapes are very beautiful, purple and finely formed like an inverted pyramid. The sun streamed through the leaves. We filled two large trailers with grapes that morning, more than they had ever picked in previous years. There was an unspoken rivalry between my English friend and me and the group of local pickers. Neither wanted to admit to thirst or exhaustion. We were also spurred on by the two girls in the party, who worked on the other side of the vines to us. As we picked, we caught sight of them leaning over the vines, a bucolic vision indeed. My colleague was so excited by this that he started lobbing grapes at one of the girls, until her boyfriend noticed and began to give us both evil looks.

Jean-Claude Mas came by briefly in his four-wheel drive. He looked at the grapes, tested their alcohol level, and declined my offer of a pair of secateurs to take part in the picking. He told me that he had decided to buy Gilles de Latude's wine crop, and had to go over there to see how the harvest was going. He departed in a cloud of dust, and we resumed our work.

Finally it was 12 o'clock. The trailer had departed with its load of grapes. We stood up for the first time in hours.

It was time for lunch. We limped up to the house, washed our hands and knocked the accumulated grime from our clothes. Under a mulberry tree, Peter had laid out a magnificent lunch of cold meat, goat's cheese and pears. He appeared in the doorway, freshly scrubbed and smelling of aftershave.

'Ah, how I have missed this year's picking,' he said. 'I adore the smell of the grapes and the sight of the sun through the leaves. Would you care for a glass of wine?'

Note: Good news reaches me: as well as continuing to sell their grapes to Jean-Claude, Gilles and Ruth have started to make their own wine called Les Trois Poules. In an innovative combination of tourism and opportunism, Ruth is persuading some of her holidaymakers to help her pick her grapes. By all accounts it is a great success. Gilles, meanwhile, is busy with his dogs and says the hunting is good!

Chez Tcheppe, Bouzigues, April 2002

Oysters in Bouzigues – a dog called Terroir –
Liebling never late for lunch – where to eat on the
beach – the Princes of Conti and a ceramic Madonna –
Clive's pies – meeting with a famous artist –
Herbert Kagley saves the world

YOU DON'T MUCH LIKE oysters, do you? It's strange, but I don't know many women that do. What is it, the fear of the aphrodisiac, or just the taste? Perhaps that is why you only had one child. I admit they don't look that appetising. But here on the banks of the Etang de Thau, in the little fishing village of Bouzigues, I am eating them as fast as they can open them. This is the last month with an 'R' in it, and I am anxious to consume as many as I can before the onset of May. It is a slightly cloudy day, for which I am grateful, although when the clouds clear, the sun beats down fiercely.

The oysters are best when the water of the Etang is cool. Soon the weather and the water will warm up, and the oysters won't taste so good. They will become cloudy with thousands of tiny sperms and eggs. People keep eating them all summer, but I prefer them as a seasonal dish, a treat for the autumn, winter and spring. They are served on large platters, a dozen at a time. You can douse them in wine vinegar, but I prefer a squeeze of lemon, just enough to make them squirm, then you loosen them from the shell, and swallow them, but not before a quick chew to extract the flavour. They taste of the sea, but without the salt.

Before this lunch, we visited Chez Tcheppe's oyster factory. The oyster beds stretch throughout much of the north coast of the Etang, big solid structures like giant sunloungers. The Etang is an estuary, about 18 kilometres long and five wide. In places it is quite shallow. Nowhere is it more than five metres deep. The baby oysters are brought in from the Atlantic coast, allowed to grow a little in tanks, and then stuck with cement onto long strips of rope. These are taken to the beds, where they hang in the water for up to nine months, when they are taken out, and sold. The industry began here about a hundred years ago. Originally, they used to breed the oysters here as well, but there was an infection and this is no longer possible.

Inside the oyster factory – a small shed with a railway line leading to the water, along which the oysters travel in small carriages – there is a woman separating the oysters and mussels from the rope. In another corner a man is cementing small oysters onto another rope. The cycle is continuous. As you sow, so must you reap. As he is working, the man is explaining the business to us, and then he shows us how to open the oysters.

With a sharp knife, he holds the oyster in his left hand and the knife in his right. He inserts the knife about a third of the way up the oyster, then moves it up and down, rather than twisting it as I always do. His movement breaks the hinge, and the oyster shell opens without any fuss or struggle. He makes it look easy. When I do it I end up with cracked shells and knife stabs in my hand. You can spot the oyster enthusiasts at parties because of these marks like stigmata on their hands. 'The terroir is very important,' he says. 'Not all the oyster beds are the same. The depth can make the water colder, which means the oysters grow more slowly. There are channels and currents. Just like with wine, some areas of the Etang are better for producing good oysters than other areas.'

I am slightly sceptical of this French notion of terroir. It is not just the ground below, but also the sky above. The best translation of it would be 'environment'. I notice that it is people who have classified terroir who talk of its importance. Wine makers claim that a metre of soil can make a difference between a great bottle of wine and a bad one. Perhaps they are right. Tcheppe claims to have good terroir. Certainly his oysters taste very good. And the price is pleasing, a tenth of what you would pay in London.

On the topic of terroir, I stopped the other day to buy some wine from the Domaine de la Colombette. It is just to the north of Béziers. A father and son run the estate and make the wine. The father has not much hair but an impressive bushy beard and the son – I guess aged about 30 – has long hair tied back. We arrived unannounced around 12 o'clock. The son, called Vincent, gave us a tasting and we bought some excellent Sauvignon Blanc, some rosé and an exotic-tasting red wine made from a grape variety called Lledoner Pelut. It tasted rich and deep and Spanish. I long to drink it with some food. Anyway, Vincent had a nice furry dog with eyes brown as Maltesers. Wine makers often call their dogs by revealing names – Jean-Luc Colombo, for example, called his retriever Haut-Brion, after one of the most famous wines in Bordeaux – so I asked Vincent the name of the dog.

'He is called Terroir,' he said. 'When we started making wine, and winning prizes with our Chardonnay, people said to us that we must have exceptional terroir. But in fact, we don't. We are on the plain of Béziers, that in the past was renowned for its quantity, not its quality. We manage to create good wine by careful work in the vineyard and the cellar.'

Now though, assuming the dog is obedient, he can boast that he has 'good terroir'.

Generally on matters of French cuisine I defer to AJ Liebling. I am told by my learned friends that I should read Brillat-Savarin's *Physiologie du Goût*, but I prefer Liebling. Liebling was an American who spent a year in Paris in the 1920s. Instead of hanging out with Hemingway, Gertrude Stein and Picasso, he sought the company of waiters, chefs and sommeliers. In later years Liebling returned to America, where he wrote for the *New Yorker*. But he wrote a memoir of his time in Paris called *Between Meals*, which describes his heroic feats of eating. Judging by the cover photograph of him, fat and well fed, clutching a bottle of wine, it does not look like he spent much time between meals. At least he was never late for lunch.

Liebling's father was a rich furrier, who indulged his son and gave him an allowance of $200 a month to spend in Paris. With each dollar worth 26 francs, one could dine well for two dollars. Liebling made the acquaintance of a theatre director, Yves Mirande, who at the age of 80 thought nothing of polishing off a lunch of 'Bayonne ham and fresh figs, a hot sausage in crust, spindles of filleted pike in a rich rose sauce Nantua, a leg of lamb larded with anchovies, artichokes on a pedestal of foie gras, and four or five kinds of cheese, with a good bottle of Bordeaux and one of Champagne, after which he would call for the Armagnac and remind Madame to have ready for dinner the larks and ortolans she had promised him, with a few langoustes and a turbot, and, of course, a fine civet made from the marcassin, or young wild boar, that the lover of the leading lady in his current production had sent up from his estate in the Sologne'.

Such heroic eating inspired the young Liebling. The book has a classic beginning, in which he recounts the famous story of how Proust bit into a Madeleine cake and was propelled back into his childhood. A Madeleine is a small cake made of sponge. Liebling imagines what Proust could have written if he had been fed properly.

'On a dozen Gardiners Island oysters, a bowl of clam chowder, a peck of steamers, some bay scallops, three sautéed soft-shelled crabs, a few ears of fresh-picked corn, a thin swordfish steak of generous area, a pair of lobsters, and a Long Island duck, he might have written a masterpiece.'

Alas, Liebling did not write a masterpiece himself, despite having the food to fortify him. If Oscar Wilde can be said to have put his genius into his life, Liebling put his genius into his stomach. His memoir of his hand-to-mouth existence in Paris is a tasty morsel that makes one regret that he did not write more.

It is hard to eat on such a grand scale down in the Languedoc, even though its most famous regional dish, cassoulet, is a colossal mixture of haricots blancs, duck, and sausage. The precise ingredients are the subject of much debate by pedants centred around the town of Castelnaudary. To eat cassoulet is the culinary equivalent of running across a ploughed field: you set off in high spirits. Half way across you are weighed down by large clods of mud; you wonder why you started on this mission; you can go neither forward nor back; in desperation you trudge on, more out of duty than pleasure.

Liebling was more fond of wine than running. Even

though wine from the Languedoc did not feature on Parisian menus in the 1920s, being an area producing solely vin de pays in those days, Liebling would drink a rosé wine called Tavel when he could afford it. It comes from the Rhône, which is quite near. It is no longer as fashionable as it was, being dismissed nowadays as unremarkable. Poor Liebling: the food he loved is too heavy. The wine too light.

In an effort to emulate the great American, I went to the Jardin des Sens, the three-starred Michelin restaurant in Montpellier. Liebling is quite scathing of Michelin guides, not on the strength of their recommendations, but because by encouraging people to travel by motorcar, they made restaurateurs lazy. They learnt they could rely on passing trade.

We had an eight-course luncheon, but some of the courses were so slight that Liebling would have been shocked, even scornful. We started with a number of amuses gueule, followed by grilled rougets, calamary with coriander, a roast pigeon's breast, an enormous cheese trolley, assorted puddings and a cup of coffee. It is run by twin brothers, known as the Frères Pourcel. Not yet 40, they have also opened a brasserie called the Compagnie des Comptoirs, where I have eaten three times, but never well; and one on the beach near La Grande Motte called Compagnie des Comptoirs Plage, where I have eaten well every time. It is by far the most stylish place to dine down here in the summer.

In Bouzigues I love the food and the view from Le Jardin de la Mer, even if the décor needs an upgrade and the service can be painfully slow. More stylish is Chez Philippe in Marseillan, with a fine wine list that is also excellent value. Also in Marseillan is the Château du Port. This is the biggest building in Marseillan, which used to be the home of the family that ran Noilly Prat. It is like a 19th-century Parisian mansion that has been rather incongruously transported to the seaside. The owners are charming and now that the road outside has been closed, you can sit by the quayside without fear of being run over or gassed by fumes.

Further inland, Le Mimosa is a treat, even if the atmosphere can be a bit sepulchral and the prices are becoming extravagant. It is run by a Welshman and his wife, who used to be a ballet dancer. Le Pressoir in Saint Saturnin and L'Horloge in Montpeyroux can be good. There is a fine restaurant in Neffies, where they prepare steak tartare in the traditional manner in front of you. There are only two places to eat in Pézenas: Le Palmier, set in an open air courtyard, with palm trees naturally, Moroccan flavours and often music to match; and Les Marronniers. This is on the other side of town near the antique shops. In the winter you can settle in the snug room with a hearty stew and a good bottle of wine. In the summer you eat outside, under the chestnut trees.

Even if you don't go out, to eat really well you don't need to cook. Most of the butchers have a plat du jour, which you can take home and heat up. Or you can buy cold food. The fresh local produce is superb. Each village has its own market days. In Laurens, for example, it is every Thursday. Here will gather a bread van, a meat van, perhaps a greengrocer, and certainly anybody that wants to sell a few tomatoes or melons. You don't even need to wait for market days to buy locally produced food. In the summer, stalls mysteriously appear in people's garages or by the side of the road. Suddenly you will discover a supply of asparagus that is better and cheaper than anything that you could buy in a formal market. But one day the stall disappears, turns back into a car parking space, so that you wonder whether it wasn't a mirage and never existed. Down the backstreets of villages, little old ladies sell bunches of onions, tomatoes and courgettes. They never fail to give you a little bunch of parsley. And once the melon season is in full flow, they are for sale everywhere.

Pézenas is our nearest big market town. It was once the centre of this part of the Languedoc, owing partly to its position on the road from Provence to Spain, partly because the Counts of Conti made their court here, but also because it picked the right side during the religious wars. Its neighbour down the road, Montagnac, sided with the protestants and has lived in woeful obscurity ever since, although it has a good market on a Friday morning.

Saturday is market day in Pézenas. You start at the fountain at the top of Cours Jean Jaurès, by a rather ghoulish memorial to the French war dead. It used to be called Cours Molière, but adoring socialists changed the name to honour the man assassinated in Paris three days before the start of the Great War. The French are very good at honouring dead politicians, perhaps to inspire people in the way that the English used to shoot admirals to encourage the sailors. In a number of towns I have stumbled across a Place Gambetta, and been amused to notice that the inhabitants have named their most important square after a prawn. It is only recently that I learned that Gambetta was another of these deceased politicians, honoured, then neglected.

The merchants gather at the top by the fountain. The first van you see is the fish van, with langoustines, crayfish still moving in a bucket, sea snails, prawns, live crabs, doomed to move sideways into pans of boiling water, large fish pies, the head of a swordfish, the sword pointing in the air like the gnomon of a sundial, turbot, mackerel, and boxes of sardines and anchovies, both shipped up from the port of Collioure. There are some shellfish stalls here too, selling oysters and mussels. On the opposite side of the street there is a lorry full of chickens turning on spits, thus ensuring that the whole town can eat a freshly roasted bird for around six euros each.

Next to this is a stall consisting of two large saucepans, one making paella, the other lamb chops, to be served with couscous. Then there is the bread stall, with a bewildering array of loaves from the mountains. Further down the concourse are massed the meat lorries, portable butcher's shops, full of hams, pâtés, boudin noir (the black blood pudding), chops and other cuts of meat. You can also find wild boar salami. Then there are goat cheese stalls, olives and pickles, huge barrels containing a hundred-weight of olives each. Beside these on the left is the cheese lady. She has a fine selection of cheeses, including Manchego from Spain, Swiss Emmenthal, Italian Parmesan and any number of French cheeses from Les Templiers to Cantal Entre Deux. She always gives Olivia a large slice of cheese to chew on while she takes our order.

After this the market takes on a rather prosaic turn, moving from food to clothes, although there is a dazzling selection of sweets including liquorice, carambars, crocodiles, fried eggs, schtroumpfs and cherry bottles. Among the clothes and shoe stalls can be found a stall selling bras in boxes; straw bags and wallpaper in Provencal patterns. If you take a left turn here, by the Porte de Faugères, you pass through a gateway, which is the last remaining entrance of the medieval town.

Pézenas's golden age lasted for nearly two centuries, peaking in the 1650s. Because of its clement climate – it manages to miss out on the Mistral and the Tramontane, and seldom snows or freezes in the winter – and its location between the mountains and the sea, the Dukes of Montmorency and then later the Princes of Conti, both governors of the Languedoc, decided that this was a good place to make their court. They brought with them nobles, camp followers, actors and artisans, who between them created more than 40 palaces of stunning design and proportions. As you pass through the Porte de Faugères the first thing you notice to the left is the old Jewish quarter, with two gates at each side of an entrance, one to protect the inhabitants and the other to protect the Jews. The Jews were thrown out of France in 1398, but only after they had contributed to the intellectual debate of the region, helping to bring Arab mathematics to the area.

The steep narrow road ahead leads to the remains of the castle, destroyed by Cardinal Richelieu in 1632, after the defeat and decapitation of Henri II of Montmorency. His domaines and power were handed to the Princes of Conti. The road itself, apart from a layer of tarmac, is virtually unchanged since medieval times. Small houses crowd both sides of the street, so you feel you could almost be in Siena. At the top of the little hill where the château used to stand is a garden, the entrance of which is locked. There are grand plans to renovate the area, and indeed there is a large list of contractors and engineers and architects, but I have never seen anyone doing any work, nor is it clear when the gardens are supposed to open.

Just past the château are the remains of the old prison, which is being turned into apartments. On a wall to the right is a ceramic Madonna. Until recently it was open to the elements and had seemingly survived 600 years or so in rain and shine, but the latest owners of the house have housed her in a glass case. Near here you will find the Musée des Portes. This is as unusual a museum as it sounds: it contains nothing but doors, door handles and architraves. It appears a place to miss even on a rainy day. But such is the quality of the exhibits that you come away enthralled. Besides, the museum is very small.

Turning right and heading downhill brings you to the heart of the old town, to Place Gambetta. This is a place to while away summer evenings, while swallows fly overhead. Sometimes there are open-air concerts here. There are often musicians, aiming to pick up a bit of tax-free cash. The quality of the playing is so good that you don't resent throwing something in the hat. Around here are a number of the palaces that were constructed by the camp followers. Hotel de Ribes at the top of rue Triperie-Vieille is one of the more exotic. Through a vaulted entrance you come out in a small courtyard. The staircase to your left is a riot of arches, columns and balustrades. The balustrades are square, not round, the work of travelling Italian artisans. Pot plants trail a stream of leaves, hanging down like a courtesan's hair. This is just the sort of place you would expect to see Romeo serenading Juliet before she is summoned indoors by the vexatious nurse.

After this detour, you can rejoin the market. It is only down at the second fountain, almost in the centre of town, that things get interesting again. Here are the flower stalls. On a good day you can smell them before you see them. Then there are pot plants, herbs and bulbs. The vegetables are here too. There is a big stall clustered round the fountain with produce brought up from Spain. At certain times of the year green beans will be piled high, or peaches, tomatoes and lettuce. Inside the cordon of traditional greengrocers, with their figs and onions, shallots and fruit, are a number of local gardeners who sell their crop almost directly from the trees. The signs are handwritten, advertising peaches or pears, and melons in season. This is where the locals shop, here and in M. Clerc's, the épicier with the shop opposite the oyster stalls.

Jean-Luc Clerc recently celebrated 30 years in business. He is a kind and cunning man, with an eye for the ladies and a handshake for the men. Once we got to know him he began offering me a cup of coffee or once, memorably and refreshingly, a cold bottle of Perrier at the height of summer after a game of tennis. His shop is everything a grocer's should be: the smell of roasted coffee, which he grinds himself in a variety of blends; excellent cheeses and hams; vegetables; preserves; and a fridge full of drinks.

One of the things I love about the market is how it changes with the seasons. In midsummer it is packed with tourists, buying straw bags to take home and eating sweets in the street. As winter comes they disappear, as does the fruit. This is replaced by Christmas fare such as oysters, game birds and ducks. Then there is the excitement of the first asparagus of the season. It begins in March and continues for a couple of months. Big bunches of asparagus spears, lightly cooked in water and eaten with olive oil, salt and pepper, and a dash of vinaigrette. Then there are the mirabelles – small green plums reminiscent of greengages. They are indigenous to Pézenas and were a major crop in the 19th century, so popular that they were packed into wooden boxes and sent to England. There is also the first crop of peaches, white and yellow, grown in the local gardens.

There is another thing that is peculiar to Pézenas. Les Petits Pâtés de Pézenas are small pastries filled with a spiced mincemeat that taste rather like the original mince pies that were eaten at Christmas. They are named after Clive of India, who rather improbably came here on holiday back in 1768. He was then governor of India and one of the richest men in the world. He travelled with a considerable entourage, including a number of cooks. Before they left, one of them passed on the recipe for Clive's Pies to the locals. The tradition died out, but was revived by a local historian, and now you can buy them in most of the bakeries.

One thing that does not change is the bar where we meet after a hard morning's shopping. There are a number of bars. The Café du Midi is the rugby bar. This is the loudest, smokiest, most fun bar in town, where the accents are thick and the coffee tastes like treacle. This is one of the few bars that stays open late in the evenings. Another bar is the Café des Arts, run by a rather unfriendly couple. The English seem to like this bar, mainly because you can sit outside in the sunshine. Here you can hear them discussing such exciting matters as the price of property or whether or not tomorrow will be a red electricity day.

Electricité de France, with devilish ingenuity, has developed a device that you place in a prominent location somewhere in the house. Each day in the winter is given a different colour code, either red, white or blue. They relate to the cost of electricity. Blue days are cheap; white days are a bit more expensive; red days are positively ruinous. However, red days are the days that you want to have the heating on. So for misers and pensioners, this system brings misery. But accountants and similar bean counters must love it.

For the first year and a half Electricité de France did not bother us at all. We did not receive a bill, nor did we pay one. Marvellous, we thought, not only is the water free, but so is the electricity. This happy situation continued until one black day when a little blue Electricité de France van turned up and cut us off. They only agreed to reinstate the supply if we would agree to pay by direct debit. Then, on one of the few days when there was money in the account, they plundered it. Worst of all, they insisted we install one of the colour-coded meters. It sat blinking at us for a day, until we turned it off and hid it in the cupboard. It would have given us something to talk about in the Café des Arts, but I don't go there.

My favourite café is the Vacassy, down past the oyster stall, but not so far down as the Molière, the café by the car park where all the tourists gather. The café is run by a husband and wife, and their furry dog. The dog is about 16 years old. Every day he walks up and down the bar, dodging the children who try to pull his tail. In the summer months there are a couple of local girls to wait on the tables outside, but for most of the year they do the work themselves. The patron serves the best coffee in town, cold beer, and an assortment of strange-coloured liqueurs that I have never dared to touch. The interior is simple: a stainless steel bar, green walls, and a number of chairs and tables, none of which is very elegant, but none of them offensive. The chairs outside may be made of plastic, but it is a green plastic, not the mind-numbing white. We talk about the rugby; the source at Sainte Cécile – as a young man the owner knew our house because the village boys used the spring as a swimming pool in the summer; and wine. He knows my interest in wine and often gives me glasses to try, but generally I drink beer with him, mainly because it is something I don't do much since leaving England.

One day we met Pézenas's most famous artist, Emmanuel Flipo. We knew he was famous because he told us. He is in his forties. With him was a young girl in a black dress and a cropped hair style. She is no more than 25. All men in their 40s like to have girlfriends in their 25s. It proves to them – and the rest of the world – that they are still vital, healthy, attractive. Gulbenkian, the Armenian oil man known as Mr Five Per Cent, who bequeathed a large portion of his wealth to the city of Lisbon, where there is a modern art museum dedicated to his memory, was advised by his doctor that he should always keep an 18-year-old mistress. This sort of doctor is hard to find nowadays.

Flipo has a studio opposite the Pézenas church, where he works in the summer. It is a fabulous building, with high ceilings, old stone walls covered in portraits of former girlfriends, and a courtyard at the rear where we drank wine one evening. In the winter he goes to New York, where he impresses the Americans with his energy and his talent and his parties. The posters advertising his work say Pézenas – New York. The comparison of the two towns is not intended as a joke.

Flipo discovered that as a painter it was easy to get girls to undress. Maybe it is a subconscious desire to preserve their beauty in paint, to shock future lovers and dismay their husbands. Flipo showed us a large painting of a beautiful girl with large breasts, long limbs and a shock of pubic hair. 'I painted her one night just before a party,' he said. 'It was incredible. She took all her clothes off and lay on that sideboard.' We all looked at the sideboard, as if she might still be there. 'The painting took me about 45 minutes. I had locked the door and all my friends were outside going crazy. They were mad when they saw the painting, which is so strong and powerful, but mainly they were mad that they had not seen her naked.'

One evening after a good dinner in town we invited him and his girlfriend back to the house for a midnight swim. We drank vodka and ate pistachios, then took off our clothes and went into the pool. Only the girl stayed sitting on the steps, reluctant to bare all for a couple of journalists and a painter without a paintbrush in his hand.

Herbert Kagley is not a man one hears much of these days. But along with the inventor of the paper clip, the Sony walkman, and possibly the Sydney Opera House, he should be celebrated for his contribution to the gaiety of modern life. Herbert Kagley was a Californian who invented the mechanical olive pitter in 1933, thus making it possible to enjoy a Martini with a perfectly pitted olive.

Even though it is now grown in many parts of the world including California and Australia, the olive is the symbol of the Mediterranean. More than 2,000 years before Kagley, the Romans built stone-crushing mills called trapeti, which squeeze the juice out of an olive without cracking the stones. The Greeks used the olive as a currency. They claimed the first olive tree, saying that it was given by the goddess Athena and grown on the Acropolis. To destroy a man's olive trees was an act of war.

Lawrence Durrell described the olive as 'a taste older than meat, older than wine'. Many of the olive producers in Provence and the Languedoc were wiped out in the frosts of 1956. They switched to producing wine instead, but more than 40 years later, olive production is back in vogue.

There are as many different types of olive as there are grapes. The big difference is that all olives are green: they go black when they ripen. In contrast, green grapes remain green; red grapes remain red. Interestingly, most red grapes produce white juice. It is only when you add the skin that the juice changes colour. Thus champagne can be made from two red grapes, Pinot Noir and Pinot Meunier, but there is no contact with the skins, unless they are making rosé. Most olives are grown to make oil, but there are some types grown just for eating. Here in the south of France the most popular kind to accompany an aperitif is the Lucques. The new crop hits the shops every spring. It is green, fleshy and very tasty.

Mechanical harvesters shake the trees until the olives fall off, but by the roadside you can see people up ladders, throwing the olives onto sheets laid out on the ground. I would prefer to pick olives to grapes any day. Grape picking is hot, brutal work. In contrast, the air is cooler during the harvest and the olive trees are taller. Picking the olives is the easy bit. As far as I can make out, the confusion begins once you try to treat the olives. For a freshly picked olive is as bitter as a sloe. To turn it into a sweet-tasting object is an art. Patrick the gardener gave me the following recipe to cure the olives:

Prick each olive twice. Put in an earthenware container with salt and leave for 15 days. Stir daily. Dry. Transfer to a sealed jar containing olive oil, pepper, cloves, rosemary, bay leaves and juniper berries. Leave for a month. Eat with a glass of wine or Noilly Prat.

Unfortunately, all the olives in the garden have been eaten by birds. There is a flock of sparrows that marches from bush to bush demolishing everything in its way. Somehow, they remind me of my family. They have destroyed the pomegranates and now they have eaten all the green olives. However, there are a number of olive trees in the surrounding countryside. These olives are smaller. I picked a decent amount, brought them back into the kitchen, and told the cleaner what I was planning to do. She started shaking her head. 'Non,' she said. When she says no it is with as much force as General de Gaulle used when refusing Britain entry into Europe. 'These are black olives. You must treat them in a different way.' Her recipe is as follows:

Place the olives in an open area where they get the air. Wait until their skins have puckered up like the faces of old women. This may take a couple of weeks. Then place in a container with olive oil, herbs and seasoning. Eat with an aperitif.

These conflicting recipes left me with a bit of a dilemma. However, when there is a choice between upsetting the person who does your laundry or the person who does the lawn, it is quite simple. At a pinch the grass could remain uncut, but shirts still need to be ironed. It would be some months before we knew which recipe we should have followed. Later, when we opened the glass jars, the olives were still inedible. We went back to buying Lucques from the market. With a bottle of vodka and a bottle of Noilly Prat, our evenings are complete.

The matador's bar in Béziers, August 2002

*A bull and a cork tree – Invincible walks free – Ponce
tougher than he sounds – a wild night at the féria –
afternoon tea with a matador – the start of the hunting
season – the night of Norman's nose – a good walk
spoiled – fat Sam comes to stay*

ALONG WITH *SWALLOWS AND AMAZONS*, do you
remember we used to read *The Story of Ferdinand*? It is
the tale of a young bull that lives in Spain. All the other
bulls want to go to the bullfight in Madrid, but not
Ferdinand. He prefers to sit under a cork tree smelling the
flowers. One drawing shows him sitting under a tree
which has bunches of corks hanging from the branches.
When he is two years old, five men with 'very funny hats'
come to select a bull to take to the bullfight.

Ferdinand retires to his cork tree as usual, but has the
misfortune to sit on a bumble bee. 'Well, if you were a
bumble bee and a bull sat on you what would you do?
You would sting him. And that is just what this bee did to
Ferdinand.' The pain is so intense that he jumps and
snorts and prances around. Perfect, say the men, he's the

119

one we want and they take him to Madrid in a cart. There is a drawing of him looking like Marie Antoinette on her way in a tumbril to the guillotine. When he gets to Madrid the matadors and picadors are already scared of him.

He has acquired a savage reputation and has been nicknamed Ferdinand the Fierce. But when he gets into the centre of the ring he sits down. All he wants to do is smell the flowers in the ladies' hair. The bandilleros are angry, the picadors angrier and the matador cries because he cannot show off with his cape and his sword. Ferdinand is carted back home, where he is pictured sitting once more under his favourite cork tree.

It is the drawings that really make the book. Done in pen and ink, they are very simple. One drawing shows Ferdinand as a young bull on his way to smell the flowers. He is drawn in detail, but then there is just the outline of the hills in the distance behind him and a couple of flowers in the foreground. There is a brilliant perspective view of Madrid in the morning of the bullfight, with flags waving, erratic guttering and two vultures sitting on a tiled roof. The book was written by the American Munro Leaf, for his friend, the illustrator Robert Lawson. Leaf wrote the book in an hour, the time it takes to write all good books. He said that he wrote it for Lawson to show what he could do.

It was first published in 1936 at the height of the Spanish civil war. Critics seized on the book as a satirical attack on aggression. Hitler banned it and ordered it burnt. Stalin however took a shine to it and allowed it to be published in Poland, where it was the only non-communist book to be available in schools. Gandhi said it was his favourite book.

As a depiction of bullfighting, it is good on the details of the costumes and the ring, but absurdly romantic. Bulls rarely leave the ring alive, unless they are injured by a stray picador's spear. In the spring of 2001 a bull walked free from Nîmes arena, after the bullfighter Enrique Ponce appealed to the president to spare its life. The crowd agreed that it had shown such courage that it deserved to live. Some months later El Juli spared the life of a bull appropriately called Invincible. Not killing the bull causes some upset to traditionalists, who feel that death is an integral element of the drama. Hemingway complained that you should not bother going to a bullfight in France, because it is neither authentic nor compelling, but Nîmes is a city with an honourable tradition of bullfighting, even though locals complain that it has been taken over by Parisians. There is no bigger insult in the south of France.

As well as the three traditional southern French arenas in Nîmes, Béziers and Arles, fights are now being staged in Fréjus, while there are plans to reintroduce them to Carcassonne soon. In the south-west there are regular fights in Les Landes, Dax, Bayonne, Eauze and Vic Fezensac. There is even talk of a bullfight in the Stade de France in Paris, the scene of the French football team's

World Cup triumph in 1998. This is a golden age of bullfighting in France.

A typical crowd in Nîmes is made up of old Spanish men with fewer teeth than the bull has horns, drawing on cigars and making acerbic comments, but there are also families, with young children and babies, and a considerable number of attractive single women, dressed more as if they were going to a concert than a bullfight. They are drawn by the drama and the thrill of watching a bullfighter at close quarters. Bullfighting, although it normally ends with the death of the bull, is a closer contest than most people imagine. In each of the two bullfights I have witnessed, the matadors have been knocked to the ground. Richard Milian, in his last fight ever in Nîmes, was thrown to the ground in the first few minutes by a 500kg bull, and never really recovered his composure.

Bullfighting is cruel, but it is a wonderful spectacle, and it is honest. As one Frenchman sitting next to me in the Nîmes arena said: 'What I love about bullfighting is that there is no cheating, no trickery. It is not like football.'

At six o'clock a crowd has formed around the arena in Béziers and is pushing its way up the stairs. There is a carnival atmosphere, even though we are off to a killing. The sun is still beating down, creating enough business for the girls handing out glasses of chilled Perrier water. Loud Latin music is blaring out of one of the bars. We advance slowly, pushing against other people, who are good-natured and happy. Later in the evening you would not want to bump into anybody like this just in case they turn nasty, but now there is no trouble. Then we are in our seats – not really seats, just a hard stone ledge with a number behind it. These are good seats, even if they are uncomfortable. The arena was built as an opera house, but they couldn't get enough people to come and listen to singing, so they turned it into a bullring. We are right below the president's box. Every good matador tries to kill his bull in good view of the president. It helps to win an ear or tail if the judge can see what is happening.

There are more than six thousand people in the packed arena, expectant. All is silent except for the tolling of church bells. I am looking round at the men selling straw hats to the crowd in the cheap seats in the sun. Later they will be in the shadows, but that is a long two hours away. There is also a man selling peanuts and sweets. He hurls the small packets long distances. I was trying to work out how he got the money, when a movement caught my eye. The bull.

The first bull was brindle coloured, like a bull terrier. It charged into the ring, stopped, sniffed the air, then ran at one of the matadors who was waving a pink cape behind a wooden fence. The bull missed the cape and the matador, and the crowd cheered. Then the matador went out and made the bull look stupid again. Trumpets blared. Two men on horses, armed with spears, rode into the ring. The horses are blindfolded with red material.

They are also protected with padding, to stop the bull's horns from piercing their sides. The matador entices the bull over to one of the horses. When the bull spots the horse it charges, trying to stick its horns into the horse's flanks. As the bull does this, the man sticks his spear into the bull's back. This is designed to weaken the bull, but not to disable him. Later in the evening the picador was too enthusiastic and managed to sever a tendon, causing the bull to limp. The aficionados went mad, shouting at the president, until he called the contest a draw, and allowed the bull to leave the arena.

Once the horses have gone, it is the turn of the bandilleros. In each hand they hold a sharp stick, rather like a dart with brightly coloured feathers along the shaft. First they try to get the attention of the bull. They do this by hissing or shouting 'toro!'. When the bull notices them, he charges. The bandillero sets off running at the same time at right angles, hoping to time his run so that he can get close enough to stick the darts in the shoulder of the bull, but not so close that the bull gets him first.

By now the bull's head is lower and he is not running with the same enthusiasm. The time is right for the matador to start making a few moves with his cape. This is not a good bull. He does not run straight, nor does he look good. The matador decides to kill him quickly. He raises a sword, entices the bull to charge, then buries the sword in the bull's shoulder. The bull goes down quickly, then is given a sharp blow on the head by one of the matador's men. The crowd claps. Two horses gallop into the ring, pulling a chain. The dead bull is attached to the chain and pulled out. The crowd cheers.

We sat on our hard seats and tried to work out what all the fuss was about. This seemed a rather elaborate way to kill a bull. Butchery surely should be left to the abattoir. I did not find the death of the bull particularly shocking, but it seemed rather unnecessary. However, the next bull changed my mind on bullfighting.

It was black, muscled as a boxer, and as fast as a car. In a bullfight there are normally six bulls and three matadors. This bull was going to be killed by a young man from Béziers called Sebastian Castella. He is 19 but looks younger. In his tight blue trousers and gold tasselled jacket, he looked like he was going to the opera or Elton John's birthday party. But when the bull charged, the mood changed. The beast was so quick that it caught a horn in the sand and almost did a headstand. The matador kept yelling 'Hey, hey, hey, hey' in a curiously high-pitched voice. After the picadors and the bandileros had done their stuff, the matador went to work on the bull with his red cape. Everything seemed in order, until the bull caught the man and knocked him to the ground. The bull tried to gore him with his horns, but the assistants ran in and distracted the bull.

There is nothing so angry as a matador that gets knocked to the ground. Regardless of any pain, his pride is hurt. He had also lost a shoe in the scuffle. He kicked his other shoe off, as if to suggest that it was the shoes that had failed him. Then he went to work on the bull again. His pride led him to let the bull pass him so closely that he was brushed by its flank. But again he got too close and was knocked to the ground. The assistants rushed in once more and saved him.

Now the matador was so angry and humiliated that he had to kill the bull. Only a clean killing would do, but he bungled the first attempt. The sword hit a bone and bounced out. The matador picked up the sword and tried again. This time the sword went into the bull. The bull tottered around for a while as the assistants waved capes into its face. Then it fell to its knees and the crowd cheered. But the matador stalked out of the ring, still scowling.

It was now the turn of Enrique Ponce to enter the ring. Ponce may sound like an unfortunate name for a matador to us, but there was nothing effeminate about his appearance, except perhaps his clothing. Ernest Hemingway wrote a lot about bullfighting, much of it guff, but on matadors he said something interesting. He complained in an early essay that you cannot compare yourself to a matador. 'You cannot compete with bull-fighters on their own ground. If anywhere. The only way most husbands are able to keep any drag with their wives at all is that, first there are only a limited number of bullfighters, second there are only a limited number of wives who have ever seen bullfights.'

Helena would not go to a bullfight even if Brad Pitt were the matador and promising to take off more than a pair of bull's ears. But the girl I was with in Béziers was much taken with Enrique Ponce. She felt that his name was not an obstacle for them getting together after the fight. When I was trying to explain to somebody later about the bullfight, and saying that it is not good to be the bull, she pointed out that you do at least get very close to the matadors.

Not only was Ponce attractive, he was brilliant. He gave a master class in bullfighting that turned it from a tawdry killing into an act of much beauty. True, it ended with the death of a bull. But it seemed a noble event, not a senseless murder. A thin slim figure dressed in red and black with gold braid against a 500-kilogramme beast. There is something primeval about the event. The first thing Ponce did was to stalk to the middle of the ring and throw his hat into it. It is supposed to be good luck if the hat lands crown down. Matadors have even been known to put weights in the hat to achieve the desired effect. Ponce had no need of such chicanery. The hat landed properly, and the crowd cheered.

Bareheaded, his dark hair moving in the breeze, he looked even younger and more vulnerable. But once he got to work on the bull it was as if he had been doing it forever. The bull was sent this way and that, humbled but not humiliated. It was man's mastery over beasts. At one point Ponce had the bull breathing over him. He just turned his back on him and looked at the crowd. When the bull was finally despatched, the killing was clean. The bull went down. The crowd roared and waved white handkerchiefs. The president – after a suitably theatrical delay – awarded Ponce one of the ears. He and his entourage did a lap of honour, throwing the ear into the crowd, and returning any cushions or hats that were thrown their way. Ponce then did a peculiar sideways skip into the centre of the ring, the jig of an athelete.

The last bull was given to the young Biterrois. This time he did not get knocked down. His performance was not theatre, nor art, but was an example of one of the bravest, almost foolhardy things I have ever witnessed. It was a bit like watching a drunk performing handstands on a narrow bridge over a river. Would he overbalance? Sebastian tried everything to get himself killed or injured. He was working the bull with the cape behind his back, twitching it here to make the animal pass him on his front, twitching it there to go behind his back. One slight miss and those tight buttocks would be pierced by an enormous horn. As he went in for the kill, the old man behind me with no teeth began muttering to the bull, as he had done every time that day at this point: 'Baisse la tête. Baisse la tête.' It was a relief for everybody when the bull finally went down. The crowd waved their handkerchiefs in joy that they had not been present at a suicide and the president awarded an ear.

By now the ring was all covered in shade, but it was still

warm outside. We left the arena and met the crowd who had not been able to get tickets. They were singing and dancing. Suddenly my friend caught sight of the van taking the matadors away and ran towards it, hoping to get a view of her heroes. I decided to take her home before it got ugly.

We went back to Béziers the next evening to join in the féria. Béziers goes wild for a week in August, with street parties, flamenco dancers and bodegas, where people eat and drink and fight and dance the night away. We went back into the bullring. By now it was dark and the arena was empty, but there is a bar at the end of the ring where the bulls come out. We walked round past the stands and had to cross a pool of blood. The bar is decorated with pictures of famous bulls and fighters and packed with people, but even so, it is a bit like having a drink in a butcher's. Everybody said that today's bullfight had been better than yesterday's. The bulls were better, and the matadors responded to the challenge. It seemed strange to be discussing this in such a matter of fact way. You cannot explain bullfighting, nor can you justify it. But there is something strangely noble about it.

There is another kind of bullfighting in France. It features the smaller, nimbler black bulls of the Camargue. They are pitted against men dressed in white called razeteurs. The razeteurs' job is to take off the rosettes that are pinned to the bulls' heads. Each bull stays in the ring for no more than 15 minutes. If he has performed well, weaved and ducked his head and chased the razeteurs, he will be serenaded with the theme tune from Bizet's Carmen. But he will not be killed.

For breeders of bulls, such as Jacques Bon, who together with his wife Lucille also runs the Camargue's most stylish hotel Le Mas de Peint, a good bull is worth a lot of money and can have a long career lasting a number of seasons. 'As the bulls get more experienced, they know what the razeteurs will be trying to do, and work out ways to stop them,' says Jacques Bon. 'Sometimes a razeteur will get hurt or even killed, but it is no more dangerous than driving a car.' The best place to see this kind of bullfighting is in Arles.

At Jacques Bon's manade you can see the bulls in the fields. The countryside is not dissimilar to Romney Marsh. There are big drainage ditches and lush green fields. But the bulls are sprightlier than anything you might run into in parts of Kent. On one part of the property is Bon's own bullring. Here he and his men select the bulls with the character to fight. Most of them do not make it and end up destined to become a good-sized steak.

One afternoon I visited the manade of a young torero called Juan Bautista. I went with a French friend called Caroline. She had met him at a party and he had phoned her up. He is a slim, good-looking boy, with high cheek bones and a shy grin. I could see why she was interested in him. We arranged to meet his sword carrier in Arles, who then led us deep into the Camargue.

Bautista was sitting in his father's house, sipping Coca-Cola and waiting for tomorrow's bullfight. He is just 21. He is ranked in the top ten bullfighters in the world, even though he looks like a choir boy. He went to a bullfighting school in Arles, where he had lessons in the morning and bullfighting in the afternoon. He was just 14 when he had his novillado – his first fight – then he became an apprentice. His first professional fight was in Arles on September 10 1997. Now he has more than 200 fights a year, in Spain, France and Mexico. His biggest rival is El Juli, the David Beckham of bullfighting.

Like many sportsmen, he is surprisingly inarticulate about his business. He began because his father was interested in bullfighting. Yes, he is apprehensive, but that is part of the job, like being a racing driver. The job satisfaction comes from being in the arena, alone with the bull and the crowd. There is fear and passion when you are face to face with the bulls. Is he scared? Sometimes. You never know what the animal will do.

He only comes to life when we ask him to pose for some photographs. He leads us to the bull ring, where he stands with a pink cape and a sword. He starts making some passes with the cape. Suddenly he stops being a young man in a Ralph Lauren shirt and khakis and becomes a bullfighter, fighting for his life. His dog, a boxer, comes near, wanting to play. He puts it in his sights, waves the cape at the dog and raises the sword. Then he relaxes, smiles, and is young again.

That night we left him and drove back home. He would wake up the next morning and face two 500kg bulls in the ring in Nîmes. The most dangerous thing I would face the next day was my wife. We had a cup of coffee with a local wine maker the next day and told him who we had met. He is a lover of bullfighting and we thought he would be impressed.

'But Bautista is not a torero. He is not Spanish,' he said.

Thus do prejudices linger. At least Hemingway would have appreciated the remark. But his disdain for bullfighting in France was expressed between the world wars. Bullfighting only came properly at the end of the Second World War, with the refugees from Spain who were fleeing Franco. They sought to keep their customs alive, and to make a bit of money in the process. In Andorra, there is the strangest monument to this attempt to promote bullfighting. In the centre of Andorra La Vella, the capital, there is a large, round metal building. It was put up to host bullfights. Unfortunately, it was not a great success. Spectators could be lured to Andorra for duty-free goods, but not to watch bulls being killed. It stood empty for a number of years, before being taken over by the local municipality. It is now used for storing snow clearing equipment.

August is not just a time for killing bulls. It also marks the start of the hunting season. As well as birds of every description, the main quarry is wild boar. The wild boar is the ancestor of the domestic pig. The males can weigh up to 200kg, sporting tusks from both the lower and upper canines. They live alone. The females live in matriarchal groups called 'sounders', with groups of up to 20 living together, along with their young. They spend the days in the undergrowth, coming out at dusk to feed on whatever is available, including fields of maize, turnips and potatoes.

Some mornings the bottom of our drive looks like a guerrilla war has broken out. Everywhere you look men in camouflage jackets, tight beeches and flat caps are standing, expectant. They carry large rifles over their shoulders. In the woods you can hear the bells of their dogs, tinkle, tinkle, tinkle, ringing out with delight when they stumble across the scent. You can hear the family of wild boar crashing through the undergrowth, running for its life. Then shots ring out and occasionally you see a dead body, stretched out in the back of a pick-up truck, hard and hairy and black.

The men start gathering around seven in the morning. I see them when I go to get the bread. They are in no hurry. They are out of the house; there are no women around; that is enough. They pass round cigarettes, blowing smoke into the air in streamers. They have a reputation for heavy drinking and reckless shooting. Every season the hunters in France manage to kill a number of their own people. They race about the countryside in a convoy of Berlingo vans, keeping in touch via radio and mobile phones. At least once a month we run into a hunter who has lost his dog. One evening I took the rubbish out late at night. It was a pitch-black night with no moon. We had just come back from a very good dinner in Tourbes. I wanted to take Sam the dog for a walk and drop off the rubbish on the way. Helena was behind me, as were Hugo and Julia and their friend Lulu. Just as we got to the rubbish, there was a deep guttural bark, the most frightening noise you can imagine in the dark. I dropped the rubbish and retreated. The girls had already run back to the house and Hugo was waiting for me on the drive.

'What was that?' he said.

'I don't know. I think we should go back and have a look.'

We took the long black torch so loved by American policemen because they can beat people around the head with them.

'Are you scared?' asked Hugo.

'No,' I lied.

'I am,' he said, and put his hand in mine.

As we got closer to the dustbin, the dog barked again. I shone the torch again and there were two hunting dogs huddled in the garrigue. They were thin and mangy and stiff from too much running and the cold, but they had a loud bark. Their eyes flashed bright in the light and Hugo gripped my hand harder. They stayed there for the night. Next morning we told them in the bakery that we had the two dogs and the owner came and collected them.

This was not the most unsettling incident we have had with a dog in France. That took place during a conventional dinner party, which has now become known as The Night of Norman's Nose. The evening began comfortably enough. However, nobody who was there will ever forget it. We had invited eight people to dinner. It was the beginning of May. The weather was unsettled, something attributed to the full moon apparently. But the evening sun had appeared and we drank champagne as we waited for the final guests to show up. There was Norman, of course, an American in his 80s. He was born at the end of the First World War in Brooklyn. He still retains the accent, a broad drawl that calls for 'cawhfee' at the end of dinner. He fought in the Pacific during the Second World War, then went into the motor business. After a successful career he sold the company and took up sailing and investing in the stock market. He met Stephanie, who is an Irish writer with two children from different men. She has the brightest blue eyes you have ever seen. Norman treats the two girls as his own. He has a great love of dogs. He has two Labradors that he bestows with affection. As we waited for Peter and Dominique to arrive, along with their daughter Georgia and her husband Stefan, we drank more champagne. We were telling Norman how the dog had come with the house.

'You are very lucky,' he said. 'He's a beautiful dawg.' We agreed. Then Peter showed up. Jazzy had chewed the bottom of his shoe when they first met. Peter has borne a grudge against the dog ever since.

'I have never trusted that breed of dog,' he said. 'I would not have him in the house.' But then he does not have any dogs in the house.

The former owners of the house had explained that they were moving to an apartment in Nîmes where there wouldn't be room for a dog, and besides, Sainte Cécile is the dog's house. He is a Belgian sheepdog called Jazzy. It is curious to give a dog the same name as the command for go away or Vas-y!, but there it is. The upshot is every time you tell him to go away, he comes towards you. While outwardly obedient, he tends to do what he wants anyway.

I have never been that keen on dogs. I prefer the aloofness of cats. I don't know what the difference is between an Alsatian and a Belgian sheepdog, but Jazzy is blonder than most Alsatians I have ever met. A friend of mine years ago used to have them at his parents' farm. I always thought they looked vicious brutes. Norman Mailer attributes some of the success that Muhammad Ali had in the Rumble in the Jungle in Zaire to the fact that George Foreman arrived with a snarling Belgian shepherd on a short leash. The Belgian sheepdog was the symbol of colonial oppression: the locals immediately sided with Ali.

There is no doubt that Jazzy is a scary-looking beast, particularly when he is barking at you. The postman refuses to get out of his van. The France Telecom men were very wary of him. 'Does your dog bite?' they asked. I was reminded of the Inspector Clouseau sketch, when he asked the same question of a man, who answers no. After Clouseau has been savaged by the beast, he turns to the man in anger.

'I thought you said your dog did not bite.'

'That is not my dog,' replies the man.

But this big barking dog is now my dog, although he treats us as guests in his house. The previous owner taught him to open doors. He wanders about, opening doors at will. Unfortunately he has not been trained to close them after him. On windy days there is the banging of doors behind him as he moves through the house.

When we arrived, he was fed on a rather bland fare of dog biscuits. I added Pedigree Chum to his bowl, along with a drizzle of olive oil. Whenever we cook a chicken on the barbecue, we give him the carcass. I know that you are not supposed to give dogs chicken bones because they stick in the throat as surely as fish bones used to stick in the Queen Mother's throat, but once we had done it once the habit stuck. His coat looked thicker and lusher, as if he had just switched shampoo.

He is said to be five years old, but although his teeth are white and long he has grey hairs around his muzzle. His eyes are a bit cloudy, affected by cataracts. Because of this he can be a bit clumsy as he moves around the house. In times of excitement he sometimes knocks over Olivia, who looks around in anger, but often fails to spot the culprit. She is probably the only person in this part of France who is not wary of him. She thinks there is nothing more fun than sneaking up on him when he is asleep by the swimming pool and tweaking his ears. When he growls, she runs away, squeals with delight, and goes back for more. Most people are more circumspect. One house guest, who was memorable for the amount of food she put away, was planning to raid the fridge one evening when she spotted him in the doorway of the kitchen. Her hunger deserted her and she tiptoed back to her room.

Most Frenchmen treat him with similar caution. When we walk him down to the bar, they pass us on the other side of the road. In the bar they give him a wide berth, keeping an eye on him at all times. Down here they don't keep dogs as pets, but as guard or gun dogs. There are a few Poodles, clipped like topiary hedges, which can be seen strutting through the streets, but these are an exception.

What I have never understood about dogs is why do they never take themselves for a walk? On Jazzy's doorstep are miles of garrigue and vineyard. He cannot wait to go for a walk. If we walk the rubbish down to the bin at the end of the drive, he is beside himself with excitement. When I start to put my shoes on, he does a little dance. The sight of the daughter's buggy sends him epileptic. But why does he need me to go for a walk with him? Why can't he just wander off alone?

Maybe years of Belgian breeding have taught him to stay close to his house and his owner. In many ways it is very reassuring. When the nights draw in, he sleeps by the front door, between us and potential intruders. Even more important, he is between greedy guests and the fridge.

On The Night of Norman's Nose, dinner began with risotto. There was plenty of wine and good conversation. Jonathan Miller, a columnist for the *Sunday Times*, was entertaining one end of the table with his views on Foot and Mouth disease. At the other end of the table Norman was telling Mrs Miller his views on the New York stock market. Even though she was then chief legal counsel for Goldman Sachs in Europe, he felt she could benefit from his knowledge and experience.

I brought in a leg of lamb that I had cooked, together with some salad. We had more wine. Everybody was interested to learn which butcher in Pézenas had provided the lamb. When I told them, they seemed happy and agreed that this was the best butcher in town. I don't know what it is about France, but it turns everyone into a keen shopper and a dedicated eater.

Jazzy had seen the lamb from outside and decided that he would like a slice. I let him into the dining room and he went to greet each person in turn. Jonathan gave him a sliver of lamb. Then Jazzy went to talk to Norman.

'I can't tell you what a nice evening we are having,' said Stephanie.

It was moments later that things turned grim. If you are of a nervous disposition it would probably be advisable to look away. For Norman, having a good time, decided that he would cap it by hugging the dog and putting his nose close to his face. Unfortunately Norman is deaf in one ear. Jazzy growled into it, but he did not hear. So he bit Norman's nose. This provoked an immediate reaction. Blood started spurting from Norman's nose. And he began to scream in pain.

'Oh, oh, oh, oh,' he wailed. The people sitting next to him looked up from their conversations. Even Jonathan was momentarily silenced. Norman was in pain.

Jazzy looked rather sheepish, surprised at the reaction.

'Somebody call an ambulance,' said a shaken voice.

'Get some ice.'

'I am the son of a doctor,' said Jonathan. 'Stand aside.'

So we filled napkins with ice and Jonathan held them on Norman's nose, while a number of the guests hid in the kitchen and shook their heads. Then we noticed that there was something lying on the floor next to Norman. It could have been a bit of lamb. It could also have been a piece of Norman's nose. I got Jazzy out of the room before he decided to eat whatever it was. A couple of the women were looking green.

'Listen,' said Norman. 'It is only a scratch. I will be fine. Give me a plaster.'

Those of us who had seen the thing on the floor knew

that a plaster would not suffice. Dominique, who had been calling for an ambulance, called the hospital in Pézenas instead. Norman would be taken there. He was helped to his feet. There is a large mirror that hangs in the dining room. Norman paused to look at the damage.

'It's fine,' he said. 'There's just a bit of blood.' Nine green people looked at each other.

'I think you had better go just in case,' said Jonathan.

Norman was led away. 'Don't remonstrate with the dawg,' he said. 'It was my fault.'

There was silence as we listened to the car disappear down the drive.

'I thought he was going to go into shock,' said Jonathan.

'Are you really the son of a doctor?' I asked.

'Well, he was a psychiatrist, but it's the same thing,' he said. Then he went into shock himself. His face turned pale and he kept shaking his head, muttering to himself.

There was still the business of the thing on the floor to resolve.

'I think it is a piece of lamb,' said Helena.

'It is definitely lamb,' I said.

We all knew it was Norman's nose.

'I am going to make an executive decision,' said Mrs Miller. 'It is a piece of lamb, but we don't need it lying on the floor.' She got some kitchen paper, scooped the thing into it, and threw it into the bin. Jonathan started rocking violently.

'Glass of wine?' I asked.

'I think we had better be going,' chorused everybody.

Stephanie, Georgia and Dominique had all departed with Norman to the hospital. Peter was keen to get out of the house before the dog decided on a second course. I was keen to get Jonathan out of the house before he was sick.

'Oh well,' said Mrs Miller. 'C'est la vie.'

If this incident was not bad enough, there was then the business of what to do with the dog. Up to that moment, the dog had been a pretty good friend. It is true that he had bitten a forester, frightened Julia and put the wind up Helena's mother, chased a jogger into a ditch and threatened to kill the postman every morning, but these were isolated incidents. He kept any marauding petty thieves away from the property and warned us while we were swimming naked in the pool that there was somebody at the door. But there was no escaping the fact that there is a contract between man and dog: man feeds dog; dog does not bite man's dinner guests. Jazzy had broken this rule. His contract would have to be terminated.

We tried to find somebody who might like to give him a new home, but nobody was interested. Then there was a groundswell of public opinion in favour of keeping the dog. I wanted to keep him. He was as good a dog as you could hope for, as good a dog as ever bit anybody's nose. But then he tried to bite Olivia. We cannot be sure that he tried to bite Olivia, but the Swedish au pair said that he did. She had been pretty sure that there was only one thing to do with Jazzy. We had discussed the incident the next morning over breakfast.

'The problem is what do we do with Jazzy,' I said.

'I would have thought as a parent that there is only one thing to do with Jazzy,' she said, sternly. They may look sweet, these Swedish au pairs, but they have a dark side.

So I phoned up a vet and told him of my plan to send Jazzy to the great dog basket in the sky.

'Eez not possible,' he said. 'You don't have the right.'

'Why not?'

'He must be put under surveillance.'

'Why?'

'How many has he bitten, will he bite people again?'

'Who knows?' I said.

'What is your name?'

I hung up. Later Helena phoned a vet who told us that the procedure is that you have to take the dog to a vet three times before they will despatch him. It is a case of third time unlucky for the dog. I thought it was quite unfair to take him backwards and forwards in a car. I also knew that the longer we delayed, the worse it would get. So I went to a neighbour and borrowed a gun. It was a nine millimetre, not the ideal tool for what we had in mind, but better than nothing. There were pictures of songbirds on the cover of the box of cartridges, but I did not feel like singing.

Then we set off for a final walk. There was my brother, Jazzy and me. I kept thinking of the scene in the film

Lawrence of Arabia after there had been a fight in the camp. The only way to resolve the feud between the two factions is for Lawrence to kill the man who has murdered somebody else. Lawrence agrees to do it in the hope of uniting his forces. But when he meets the murderer, he discovers that it is his friend, the boy who fell off his camel in a sandstorm, forcing Lawrence to ride back and save him. Now there is no choice. If he saves the boy's life again his army will disperse. He will never get to Damascus. Lawrence pulls out his revolver. His hand shakes. He shoots him dead.

We walked on, past the vineyards and into the area of garrigue that the children and I had christened 'Jazzy's Jungle'. Cecil Rhodes, the great African pioneer is buried in a piece of land in the Matopos Hills called 'World's View'. He had chosen it as his burial site. It is a magnificent spot: there are views over Bulawayo, strange coloured lizards climb the granite rocks, and there is a sense that if one had to be buried anywhere, this would do. I had planned to take Jazzy to a similar spot, a rocky site so that he would not be dug up by a hungry boar, with a view over the hills he loved.

He ran through the garrigue for the last time, his nose brushing my hand, his feet catching my heels. I knew that on my own I would not be able to kill him. But I also knew that life at Sainte Cécile would no longer be settled all the while he was around. So at the top of the hill I put him between knees, my brother put the barrel next to the back of his head and pulled the trigger. Jazzy fell silently to the ground. His body twitched, but he had not felt a thing. One minute he was enjoying a walk, the next minute his life was over. As a way to die it beats many others. I certainly felt it beat being carted backwards and forwards to the vet, finally being given a lethal injection like a mass murderer on death row.

We made a space in the rocks and covered his body. His resting place is like the tomb of a neolithic man, a dolmen. Then we walked back down the path, horribly affected by what had happened but knowing it was the right decision. There were still marks where he had lain next to the wall with his damp coat and it was horrible to see the smug expression of the postman next day. I felt like shooting him.

To ease the loss of the dog we decided to get another one immediately. People cautioned against it. 'Take a bit of time to decide,' they said, but foolishly we ignored them. The idea of a dog when you live in a house surrounded just by vineyards is comforting. I had enjoyed taking Jazzy on evening walks, looking at the stars and the glow-worms in the hedges. Perhaps the new dog would be just as much fun, without the pain. So we looked in the local paper and found somebody advertising Labrador puppies in the hills up by Olargues, a pretty medieval town full of bridges. There was only one bitch, which made choosing which dog to have much easier. We drove up there one evening and drove away with the golden Labrador puppy. She snuggled in between Helena's neck and shoulder all the way home and did not make a fuss. When we got her back to the house it was as if she had always lived here. She ate some food quickly, then chased the cat.

I don't think I have ever met a greedier living creature. She is the AJ Liebling of dogs. Her face hits the food and it's gone. When she is not eating, she is looking for more food. And she bites everybody, other dogs, the children. We gave her to my daughter Julia as a birthday present. Julia lives most of the time in London. What she wanted most in the world is a dog, but because there is not much space in London and her mother is brighter than me, a dog has been vetoed. So Julia has a dog, without the pain of looking after it. Which suits her fine. Her previous pet was a goldfish. It became ill, so drugs were poured in the bowl. The goldfish perked up no end, swam round the bowl like a killer shark for five minutes, then died. Ten days later, Julia asked how the goldfish was.

She named the dog Sugar. In France, the name of every pedigree dog of a certain breed born in the same year must begin with the same letter. Sugar is as good a name as any, although there have been times when I have called her other things beginning with the letter S. But before Julia came down to France to name her birthday present, the Swedish au pair started to call her Valpen, which is Swedish for puppy, which stuck for a while, until one evening I was reading the children Dr Seuss's *Green Eggs and Ham*. 'I do not like that Sam I am,' we all chorused. And then we realised that none of us liked the dog either, so we called her Sam.

Norman had warned us that she would eat things. 'You'd be amazed the things she can destroy of value,' he said. To date she has gone through a pair of blue cushions, Gucci sunglasses, a mobile phone, a phone charger, three pairs of shoes, two cuddly toys, a hairbrush, a novel by Martin Amis that a house guest had left behind (apparently the dog found it indigestible too), a toaster, a boxed CD set of Jacqueline du Pré's cello playing, Hugo's collection of marbles, Julia's favourite teddy bear, a Hewlett Packard printer, a billiard cue, a tennis racket, a table tennis bat and a box of balls, any food left anywhere, and an alarm clock. But we are finally beginning to like her, even though she has some strange habits. She eats snails, chewing them as a schoolboy eats Smarties, but I guess that is what you would expect from a French dog. You can hear from the way she attacks them that she likes them crunchy on the outside, chewy on the inside. She is also very fond of grapes, grabbing them from vines as we walk through the vineyards. But as each vineyard is full of 5,000 bunches, I don't think they will miss the odd one. She likes to have an afternoon kip in one of the sunloungers, the hammock or the rocking chair. Or an early morning dip in the swimming pool. When you turf her out she looks aggrieved, shocked that you think she is unsuitable for such luxury.

Point Zéro, La Grande Motte, October 2002

> A white ram on the beach –
> fleecing the peasants, spraying
> the beaches – bastards in caps – Point
> Zéro – the Tour de Constance – buying a
> boat – sailing up the Hérault – stuck in
> Sète – running aground – a night
> rescue – a place called La Clape

ANOTHER SUMMER HAS GONE by, the swallows are gathering on the telegraph wires, but you still haven't come down to see us. Why? This is one of the best months to be in the Languedoc. The visitors have gone, leaving only footprints and empty water bottles on the beach, but there are still a few restaurants open and they are grateful for any business. It can still be warm, but it is pleasant. Yesterday we drove down past Montpellier to La Grande Motte, one of the most unusual beach resorts in France.

It was 43 years ago, in August 1962, that Jean Balladur first visited the beach at La Grande Motte. La Grande Motte was a vineyard, with a charming old farmhouse with grey shutters and a wooden table outside and sand dunes leading to the water. There is a photo that Balladur took on his first visit of the sign, Domaine Grande Motte, sunbleached and propped against a post that carries the message 'Chasse Gardée'. There is nothing else in the photo except scrubland, some sparse trees in the distance, and a couple of old Citroën cars. Balladur was visiting the beach after receiving an unexpected letter from the Minister of Construction, Jacques Maziol. The government of Charles de Gaulle had decided to develop the coast of Languedoc Roussillon for tourism. Would Balladur care to get involved?

Balladur had been a brilliant student, and as a young man had considered being either a poet or a musician. He studied under Jean-Paul Sartre and became the philosopher's protégé. He started writing essays on architecture in the magazine *Les Temps Modernes*, and by 1962 had completed several architectural projects including a business centre, the seat of the Curie Foundation and a villa. When he received the letter inviting him to develop a beach resort he was holidaying with his family on the Côte d'Azur. Before replying to the ministry he decided to drive along the coast and take a closer look. He admits that his knowledge of the Languedoc Roussillon region was slight, except for the pictures he had seen of the Maison Carrée in Nîmes, the Roman temple, and the cathedral Saint-Pierre in Montpellier. But his heart leapt at the idea of getting involved in such a vast project. He was just 40, the age when people begin to concentrate on working before it is too late.

The family drove up from Sainte Maxime, a pretty seaside village just across the bay from St Tropez. They turned off at Grau-du-Roi, and saw for the first time the beaches and dunes, left to the mercy of the sea and the wind, infested with mosquitoes, and covered by a thin carpet of stunted plants. The contrast with the countryside of the Côte d'Azur could not have been keener. The expressions of his wife and family echoed his own concerns. He realised that this would be a much greater undertaking than he had imagined.

They parked the car and walked along the windswept beach. Suddenly a solitary horseman, dressed in black, appeared over the dunes. He rode onto the beach accompanied by a single white ram wearing a collar and passed the family without a word. It was this strange encounter with these silent creatures that persuaded Balladur, then and there on the beach, to say yes to the invitation from the ministry, even though it would mean changing the way of life of the solitary horseman and his animals forever.

Planning began in secret, although it is hard to see how the locals could not have suspected that something was up when they saw Parisians in tight black suits and highly polished shoes walking over the dunes. Secrecy was paramount to keep the cost of buying the land to a minimum. Once a decent amount of land had been bought, this would set a precedent for further purchases. But if news leaked out, it would encourage speculators. So they approached the owner of La Grande Motte and persuaded him to sell some useless land – boggy and swampland and parcels of beach – for less than a franc a square metre. He probably thought that he was being quite cunning in disposing of this land at such a good price. What he did not realise was that this price would set a precedent for further purchases, which would be compulsory. Poor Monsieur Grassion.

While this peasant was being fleeced, Balladur was sketching among the dunes. He was keen to hear from the site itself what it wanted to see built. Balladur, don't forget, had studied with Sartre. He believed that a place is a person. He quotes the line from the poem by Mallarmé: 'Rien n'aura eu lieu que le lieu.'

Balladur's belief is that architects do not make a sufficient study of the land before coming up with their designs. Sitting in front of a drawing board in a darkened office is no substitute for being in the place itself, looking at the view and the sky and the water. Balladur's reveries convinced him that his buildings should be in the shape of a pyramid, echoing the shape of the Pic St Loup, the tooth-like mountain that dominates in the distance. He travelled to the temple of Téotihuacan in Mexico, where a local architect confirmed that his thinking was sound. The temples of the Moon and Sun were planned as a symbolic reconstruction of the mountains from where the Aztecs had originally come, before they conquered the Mexican plains. He doesn't mention the pyramids of Egypt as an inspiration, which seems strange, given France's interest in all things Egyptian. All Balladur had to do was convince the others of his plans.

For the beach is a cultural necessity in France. More than half the French population holidays less than 500 metres from the coast. One hundred and fifty years earlier one only swam if one fell off a boat. Sailors tended not to be able to swim anyway, so they drowned. Then the Prince of Wales went to Brighton and swam in the sea as a health cure. The French have always been keen on spas and salt and health cures for their livers and other organs, so they adopted the practice. At first, the bathers crowded the sea shore, holding on to ropes that were attached to groynes. Then the Côte d'Azur was invented in the 1920s by a bunch of idle expatriate English and Americans. The beach becomes the stage and kingdom of Dick Diver, the hero of Scott Fitzgerald's *Tender is the Night*. When we first meet him he is raking the beach by Gausse's Hôtel des Etrangers, amusing the assembled sunbathers with his antics. When we last see him, he blesses the beach with a papal cross, before disappearing to Buffalo to molest young girls.

After the Second World War, the workers wanted to have their own holidays at the seaside. They went to the channel beaches, dressed in their Sunday best, where they were known as salopards en casquettes – bastards in caps.

The government of Charles de Gaulle decided that these workers and the middle classes needed more beaches to frolic on during the summer months. The Côte d'Azur was too crowded and too expensive; besides, which government minister wanted to lie on the beach next to his plumber? Tourism would bring jobs and money to a region of France that relied almost solely on agriculture and wine, a region in decline, which the young fled at the earliest opportunity for the cities.

Planes were sent in to spray the mosquito coast with DDT. They do it every year still, just as the mosquitoes are hatching. This programme has been successful in limiting the number of mosquitoes, but it has provoked outrage from environmentalists, who argue the natural habitat of birds and insects is suffering from the spraying. Their claims are probably incontestable. But without the efforts of the pilots, nobody would venture on to the beaches.

La Grande Motte looks every day of its 40 years. The concrete pavements have weathered badly. They were designed to look like paving slabs, but the work was shoddily completed. When you make pavements like this, you lay wood between the concrete and then pull out the pieces of wood which have acted as a frame. But in places this was done without enough care, so the edges are chipped and distressed. You wonder why they chose to do this in the first place. Were they scared of riots, of a mob in bathing costumes ripping up the paving slabs and charging the rows of mounted police? The street lamps are so much of their era they are almost a cliché: glass bowls the size of a football, mounted on metal poles. The colours also date the place. The brown that was so popular in the 1960s is everywhere, as well as bright orange, and an off-green. Each large pyramid is individual, with different patterns of moulded concrete. The best buildings are down by the port overlooking the boats. Some of them look as though they were designed using stencils, while another looks as though it was made out of egg boxes. When these were first built, they were exciting. This was a vision of the future – and to some extent it still works. The place may be vulgar, crowded and commercial, but the bathers, all crowded within 50 metres of the shore, seem happy enough, batting balls to each other, lying on lilos, or getting covered in sand. Down on the front there is a carousel, where empty horses ride round and round to the accompaniment of tinned music and flashing lights. Here there is a Place Diana, a memorial to the dead princess, but people are too busy working on their suntans to notice. This is what Jean Balladur called Point Zéro, I guess without a sense of irony, for this kind of totalitarianism is often without irony. Each restaurant and bar is tattier than the next, although there are a couple of better-looking places like Chez Antoine, as if there is a relentless attempt to take the place upmarket. It is probably destined to failure, but you have to applaud the effort.

It is a ten-minute drive along the coast to Aigues

Mortes, but it takes you back 800 years in time. The walls of the crusader stronghold rise above the marshland of the Petite Camargue like a fantasy castle, the stone throbbing in the heat of the midday sun. It was from here that the armies gathered before setting off to the Holy Land on the second and third crusades. It was built in the 13th century, by order of King Louis XI. It was his son, Philip, who commissioned Genoan stone masons to build the flamboyant walls, rather like the design of Damietta in Egypt.

The first landmark you see as you cross the bridge is the Tour de Constance, named after the King of France's daughter. The weather vane is like an arrow, a nice modern touch that echoes the thin slits of the tower. This was a building designed to last. The walls are four metres thick, made of solid grey stone. The air is cool, as if it has been inside for centuries and never seen daylight. There is a fine view from the top, over the salt flats to the south to the sea, and up the canals to the east and west. For 34 years the tower's most famous internee, Marie Durand, would have gazed out at the waters and wondered if she were ever going to be set free. Her crime was to be the daughter of a protestant preacher, who had moved to the hills of the Cevennes. This dense and remote land became a place of refuge for French protestants after the Edict of Nantes, which granted freedom of religious belief, was revoked in 1685. Many northern French emigrated to England, where they were known as Huguenots. Southern protestants, and those who could not bear the thought of English cooking, took to the hills.

It is 1,726 paces around the walls of Aigues Mortes. You walk on the ramparts, looking down at the town below and through the walls in each tower, out to the salt flats. As you get further away from the main entrance the town becomes less well developed. There are roofs caving in, barns waiting to be converted into tourist traps, but for now they are empty, except for a couple of rusting cars and a bicycle.

The best way to see the coast is from a boat. Not long after we moved to France, Helena's aunt announced that she was giving us a sailing boat. She is an eight-metre day racer, with a small cabin and beautiful lines, designed by Ron Holland. The present was not quite as grand as it sounds. The boat had been languishing in a boatyard near Rome for a couple of years. There was money to pay for the dry dock. There was also the question of how to get the boat to France. We considered sailing her, but as she had been out of the water for so long it was hard to know how seaworthy she would be. There is an engine, but that was out of the boat. Even though Helena speaks Italian, we were unable to persuade the boatyard to do any work on her. Finally we found an Italian who was prepared to load her on his lorry and drive her to Marseillan. He phoned on Monday evening from Montpellier.

'I 'ave ze boat,' he said. 'I see you tomorrow at the harbour at eight.'

Getting the small children to school and taking the bigger children to the boat yard proved a logistical nightmare, but somehow we made it to the port at eight o'clock. There was no sign of the Italian; there was no sign of the boat builder.

'You are a useless idiot,' said Helena. I wasn't quite sure why it was my fault that two Mediterraneans had failed to keep a rendezvous at eight o'clock in the morning, so I told her quite emphatically what I thought and stomped off to the café for a spot of breakfast. Helena paced up and down the quay. Hugo and Julia looked expectant, almost excited, in the hope that the argument might continue.

At nine o'clock the boatmen turned up. At nine-thirty Signor Mercati showed up. In his bright red cashmere cardigan, he could only have come from Rome. He showed more interest in Julia and Helena than where to put the boat or whether to count his money, which of course we had ready for him in cash. He reminded me of the Italian plumber who worked for us. 'Sotto la tavola, sotto la tavola,' he would chant whenever we asked how he wanted to be paid. 'Under the table.'

The boatmen unloaded the boat with the help of a rusty yellow crane and put her on blocks. She looked rather sad and unloved without her mast, which had been unstepped for the journey. The boatman said he would paint the hull. We paid Signor Mercati and left.

At regular intervals once a week we would visit the

boatyard. There was always an excuse as to why nothing had happened. Sometimes I would arrange to meet him there but somehow we never managed to coincide our visits. There was always a good reason for the lack of progress. First it was the bad weather. Then it was the pressure of work. Finally I persuaded my brother to fly out to France for a long weekend. He knows a lot about boats and engines. I thought it would be useful to have someone there who would not be fazed by either the boatman's incomprehensible French or his implied knowledge of boats. When we got to the yard there was the boat, sitting patiently now on a trailer, but nothing was happening to her. We tracked the boatman down and found him in his office. We were ready to berate him for his incompetence, laziness and sheer stupidity, when we noticed sitting on his desk was an extremely pretty girl in her 20s wearing a very short skirt. She looked at us with amusement and crossed and uncrossed her legs. We mumbled something about the boat, made our excuses and left. As far as we were concerned he had something better planned for the afternoon than sanding down a boat and we thought good luck to him.

Finally, I decided that urgent action had to be taken. I had visited with French friends, who impressed on the boatman the need for action; I had offered him money; even threatened him. Nothing worked. So in desperation I phoned Sylvain. I had been told he was the man to salvage the boat. We made an appointment to meet at the boat at nine o'clock in the morning. When I arrived there only ten minutes late, I was amazed to see a figure crawling over the boat. He jumped down, and turned out to be no taller than my waist, but with a shock of orange hair and scars from a motor bike accident.

'What a lovely boat,' he said.

'Can you fix it?'

'Sure.'

'What about the engine? The boatman tells me it is broken, that there is a piece missing.'

'Let's go and have a look at it.'

We walked over to the boatyard. Sadly the girl with the legs was no longer there, but the engine was sitting in the corner, covered in oil and grease.

'The engine looks fine. We'll take it.'

So he and a mate turned up two days later in a power boat and towed the boat to Cap d'Agde. He arranged a mooring for me, then phoned me with updates as to how the work was progressing. Then he had to go on holiday. Finally he phoned with the news that the boat would need painting and that the spare parts had been delayed. He told me on numerous occasions that the boat was a lovely boat, which he would like to buy, but when I asked him how much he would pay, he went very quiet.

'She is not worth much until she has been repaired.'

'But you could do that.'

'Non, I think it is better if you do it.'

Six months later we sailed up the Hérault like ancient

Greeks. We moored by the Tamarissière hotel. We went for a beer nearby, then had a picnic by the boat. We were going to ask Helena to name the boat and smash a glass of champagne on the hull, but just before we did that a bad-tempered woman came out of the hotel and told us not to use her mooring again. So we sailed back to Cap d'Agde.

That summer we learned to sail. I had sailed before. A girlfriend's father had kept a boat at Chichester and we sailed around the Solent, up to Buckler's Hard, where we would moor for the night and drink wine from a box. One year we raced at Cowes. Another time I joined a group of friends and we raced during Poole Harbour week. The captain would open cans of Special Brew as we were leaving the harbour. But we had the fastest boat and a couple of Australians on board, so we were seldom headed. I spent a New Year's in Sydney and we hired a boat and explored Pittwater, a fabulous area to the north, ideal for sailing. One time I even sailed with Sir Peter Blake, just a couple of years before he was shot on the Amazon. I also sailed with Luca Bassani, the creator of Wally yachts, which are the finest, most beautiful sailing boats in the world. With him we raced into Monaco harbour under full sail, caused a flotilla of small boats to scatter, then went about sharply, leaving the harbour master shaking his fist and cursing billionaires.

But there is a difference between crewing a boat and skippering it. Particularly this boat, the Margarita, which is a bit like a classic sports car. The engine is temperamental. And the skipper is prone to lapses in concentration.

It was always my ambition to moor the boat in Marseillan, which is on the Etang de Thau. I went to the capitainerie and asked whether it would be possible to have a berth.

'Ten years' waiting list,' he said. 'At least.'

This seemed a bit excessive. So I went along to the restaurant called the Château du Port, where Patricia and her lovely daughter serve up seafood during the summer. I told her of my predicament and she smiled reassuringly.

'With me it will be ten minutes,' she said.

When I went back to the capitainerie they were more helpful and put me on the waiting list, but there was still no guarantee. So I phoned ahead to reserve a visitor's berth for the night. You have to sail along the coast first, then pass through five bridges in Sète, then back through the Etang. The bridges open either around 9 o'clock in the morning or 6.45 at night. We left around 3.30. The last time I had promised to take Jean-Claude sailing the engine would not start, so I was delighted when it came to life almost immediately. He cast off the lines and we went backwards, at high speed, into a motorboat behind us. The throttle was stuck. There was an awful sound like nails on a blackboard as the newly painted hull was scratched by the propeller of the motor boat. I managed to get the boat forward, then it careered off again. Luckily I managed to head it into the dock that they use for lifting boats out of the water, then unstick the throttle and get it going forward. We got out of the harbour without further incident. The wind was good for the first 20 minutes, but then it dropped. We lazed along. On board was Helena, Jean-Claude and myself. We had a cool box with a bottle of water and a bottle of rosé wine. We passed the naturist beach. Helena was distracted by a motor boat driven by a naked man.

'Did you see his willy?' she said. 'It was rather big.'

We were too busy struggling with the wine cork to notice passers-by, however well hung. In the afternoon sun we drank the wine and dropped the cork in the water to see how fast we were moving. It bobbed along beside us for a bit, then seemed to get ahead of us. Helena announced that she needed a swim, probably to cool off after the excitement of the man in the motor boat. As we were near the nudist beach she stripped off, took hold of a length of rope, and jumped off the boat. She was pulled through the water like a salmon.

'This is great fun,' she said. We carried on down the coast, then she announced that she wanted to get back on board. Immediately we noticed a problem. There was no ladder to help lift her back on the boat. She tried to pull herself up on the rope, but that did not work. So Jean-Claude and I had to grab an arm each and pull. She popped out of the water and lay struggling for air in the cockpit.

We watched the shore. It seemed not to move. It was

now five o'clock. If we did not get there in time we would have to sail all the way back. I put the engine on. Apart from one minor mishap of steering into the middle of an oyster bed, we began to make good time. At six o'clock we could see the outskirts of Sète, rather grand houses that are built on the side of an extinct volcano. At 6.15 we were passing by the America's Cup restaurant, which sits up on a promontory overlooking the sea. We got sails down and entered the harbour at 6.30. Sylvain the boatman had shown me on the chart where to go. We rounded the harbour wall, passed the sailing boats all moored up, and headed towards one of the bridges. It was 6.40. There were no other sailing boats in sight. In fact, I had noticed one of them going in the opposite direction, but hadn't said anything. We looked at the bridge.

'That bridge is not going anywhere,' said Jean-Claude. 'I think we should go back.'

We turned the boat round and gunned the engine. We had only five minutes to get there before the bridges would open. I cut the corner and passed a couple of surprised fishermen.

'It says 6.45 on my watch,' said Helena.

Round the corner we saw a number of sailing boats milling about, as if they were waiting for something. We pulled alongside one of them, who said yes, we were in time. We were rather pleased with ourselves. Success, at last. Why don't you put the engine in reverse, said Jean-Claude. We might be able to find out what was wrong earlier. I slowed the engine, and slipped it into reverse. The engine slowed, then stopped. We were bobbing about in the busy harbour with no power. I dived below to try to start the engine. Nothing happened. I came out of the cabin to see the boats that were lined up passing serenely through the bridges before they closed. I managed to head the powerless boat towards the harbour wall and alongside a fishing boat that was moored up. We got a line on board. We were safe, but stranded. Jean-Claude walked along to the capitainerie to find out what we should do now. They told him that we should have phoned ahead that we were coming, that we couldn't stay where we were, but they couldn't help us.

Just when he was back relaying this news to us, a small motor boat with an attractive couple and a young child pulled alongside.

'You can't moor here,' he said. 'It's my fishing boat.'

We explained that we could not move. The engine was bust. He put a line on the bow and towed us to where all the sailing boats were moored. It was a pleasure to watch somebody so skilled at handling a boat. They manoeuvred our stern onto the quay, then moved up to the bows, where his wife put a rope through a buoy and tied a knot effortlessly. We were safe.

We tried the engine again. Still nothing. The battery appeared to be dead. We cleaned out the boat, took the battery out, and resolved to charge it overnight. Jean-Claude's wife Alexandra came to pick us up and we enjoyed a fine dinner in Agde. Jean-Claude had a charger and would sort out the battery for us. Next morning we got up at seven o'clock and raced back to Sète, stopping en route for the battery. We picked up some baguettes for breakfast and filled a cool box full of water and fruit. Jean-Claude could not come.

'I've got some work to do,' he said. 'I will see you later.'

The engine would not start. So we took the battery out again, left the boat bobbing in the harbour and took it back to be charged some more. We spent most of that week racing backwards and forwards, preparing for a voyage that we could not start. Sylvain the boatman gave us a new battery, but even that did not work. Eventually, the mechanic agreed to go and look at the engine. He reported that it was the starter motor that was stuck, but was now running perfectly.

Most people I knew managed to come up with a reason to be elsewhere. Helena had to dash to London; Jean-Claude was busy looking at grapes growing. So my crew that Friday night consisted of my daughter, Julia, and Caroline, an attractive 30-year-old girl who grew up in Castelnau de Gers, which is just outside Pézenas. She has a wild mane of dark hair and a voluptuous body that is always threatening to fall out of her bikini. In her you can see parts of all the people that have ever passed through the region: her nose is Arab, her hair is Visigoth, her figure Gallic. Her temper is Mediterranean.

We packed a picnic, a couple of beers and a bottle of rosé wine. We got there early, just in case. The boat had been moved from its original mooring on the edge of the pontoon into a nasty tight spot, next to a rusting giant boat that had been turned into a restaurant. Even if we got the engine going I was not sure that we could get out of the mooring, particularly in the light of what happened the last time. But the engine started first time. We turned it off and filled up the diesel tank. Then I had an argument with the harbour man, who told me that I owed him for two nights and when I went back to pay, said it was for three nights. I did not mind that he wanted me to pay for three nights, but I objected to him changing his mind without admitting that he had told me it was two nights. His friend whom we had met on the first night was more sympathetic.

'You have fixed the engine?' he asked.

'I hope so. That mooring seems rather tight. Do you think I will get out all right?'

'Yes, if you are used to boats.'

Do you remember when I was younger and you used to read all the *Swallows and Amazons* books to me? In the first one, I think it was called *Swallows and Amazons*, they ask their father whether they can go sailing. He sends back an enigmatic telegram: BETTER DROWNED THAN DUFFERS. IF NOT DUFFERS WONT DROWN. This satisfies their mother, who lets them go sailing in the Lake District.

I went back to the boat and analysed the situation. Was I a duffer? The area that I had to turn in was not much bigger than the boat. I could imagine us going backwards and forwards, smashing into boats, and the merry burghers of Sète standing up on the walls laughing themselves stupid. I wanted to avoid this. Then I had a bright idea. I put a rope to the shore, pulled the stern round so it was facing out the way we wanted to go, then slowly engaged the engine. We reversed neatly out of our mooring. We made it into the harbour without any collisions, then motored out to sea, for we still had half an hour to kill before the bridges opened. We got the sails ready, then re-entered the harbour. We got in position behind another big boat with a royal ensign and waited for the first bridge. I stilled the engine into an idling position, but remained nervous that it would stall. The cars were stopped. Two small boys sat with their legs dangling over the bridge, unseen by the harbour master. As the bridge swung sideways, they were given a free ride. Better still, we passed through the bridge and onto the next one, a high bridge that tilts up like the visor on a helmet. Two down and we were feeling pretty good. But the third bridge kept us waiting fifteen minutes. We motored around in circles, tried to avoid collisions, and drank a bottle of water. Finally this bridge opened, as did the remaining two. We were through to the Etang de Thau.

We thought about opening a bottle of champagne, but

all we had was a bottle of rosé wine. So we got the sails up first, passed by the two buoys that mark the boundary of the Etang and drank a glass of wine. There were a few other sailing boats around, but they drifted away. We were left with a good breeze and the sight of the sun setting over the hills. We cut the engine, the boat heeled over and we set a course for Marseillan. There were flying fish ahead of us and seagulls laughing all around. Then the wind died and we bobbed around. There is a concrete building on the south shore. For more than half an hour we looked at it and it looked at us, but we could not get past it. So we put the engine on, pulled the sails down, and watched the sun disappear behind the hills.

Once the sun had gone it began to get seriously dark. There were no other boats. Even the oyster beds were becoming indistinct in the gloaming. The only things we could see were a red light in the distance and a big wheel, lit up in fluorescent colours, which entertains holidaymakers. Julia complained of the cold so we gave her a jumper. Caroline kept the tiller and smoked a cigar. Then the moment came that I still find painful to remember.

We were agreed that we had left Sète behind. We knew we were far from Bouzigues. But earlier I had claimed that we had passed Mèze, the last town before Marseillan on the north shore, and Caroline was adamant that we hadn't. I allowed myself to be convinced that she was right. I think she was right. But later she managed to convince me that the town with the red light, with the church and the water tower, was also Mèze. It seemed to figure. We looked on the chart. There was the church, and yes, there was the water tower. Unfortunately, Marseillan also has a church and a water tower. We were steaming on into the night when, suddenly, the boat stopped and the engine roared. I went below, checked there was diesel. There was. But the boat would go neither backwards nor forwards. I turned the engine off. We were adrift in a dark sea, but we weren't moving. We were aground.

It is a very bad feeling to run aground in a boat. If you are stuck in a car, you can get out and assess the situation. You can find somebody to pull you out or you can walk home. But when you are in the middle of a lagoon in the dark with a child and a French woman, you are rather stuck. Julia looked rather horrified, wrapped herself up in a blanket, and fell asleep. We tried to phone the capitainerie. No answer. We phoned the boatman. No response. Finally we got hold of the French lifeboat. Yes, they had a rescue service in Mèze. Stay where you are they said, we will come and get you.

There was no prospect of us moving anywhere, so we waited. Caroline had run out of cigars so we smoked Gitanes together. They tasted horrible, but it was something to do. 'It's cold,' she said. 'Can I sit closer to you?'

Here I was, stuck on a boat, with my daughter asleep, and a French girl getting close. What should be my response? Should I go and fiddle with the engine? What would my wife think? How would she find out?

'Sure,' I said.

'It's been a long time since I have had a boyfriend,' she purred.

'Really?'

We had waited an hour when we saw a light.

'That's them,' said Caroline. She phoned them up.

'You're close. Turn your boat this way,' she ordered. The boat seemed to follow suit. But there was someone doing something odd in the bows. It did not look like a rescue boat to me.

'No, turn again,' she said.

But the boat turned the other way, then came close by. The man in the bows was sweeping with a net. As they passed us they informed us that there was not much water near where we were. Meanwhile, the rescue boat had been near us but disappeared down the other side of the Etang. We waited another hour. I began to wonder what would have happened if we had been sinking. Finally, many phone calls later, we saw two lights coming towards us. A zodiac turned up alongside containing four men in uniforms. Caroline was quite excited. She liked the look of two of them. They took off the sleeping Julia, then transferred us all into another boat that was like a trawler with a large winch. Then they put the winch rope on to the sailing boat and dragged her off the sandbed. They pointed at the light opposite from the lighthouse.

'This is not Mèze,' they said. 'This is Marseillan.'

We had motored past our destination. Feeling rather stupid, we watched as they towed the boat into Marseillan harbour. We moored up against the quay. The harbour master came out to talk to us. They were all very understanding about the fact that we were lost, did not have lights, a flare, binoculars, or any rudimentary safety equipment. Then they opened miniature bottles of spirits and wrote out a large bill that I had to promise to pay the next day.

Bitterly, I remembered the words of a friend whom I had told about the boat. 'There are only two moments of happiness in a boat owner's life,' he said. 'When you buy the boat. And when you sell it.'

A lot of the coast can be better explored either on foot or by car or best of all, from the air. The other morning Helena and I went early to a small airport near Pézenas. It has a small grassy runway, and a couple of hangars. At seven in the morning it was a still, calm day. There was still a hint of freshness in the air, and the smell of wild mint. I had come by a couple of days earlier and spoken to a man on a tractor about the possibility of a flight. He told me that he was just the tractor driver, but he could arrange it. So I wasn't surprised when I saw him towing a small plane out of the hangar onto the runway. Slightly more surprising was when he changed the tractor seat for the pilot's seat and called us to join him.

'Are you sure you can fly this thing?' I asked.

'I'll try,' he said.

We taxied to one end of the runway, then he gunned the engine and we were airborne. Suddenly below us was the town of Caux. You could clearly see the snail-shaped old town and the new houses surrounding it. Then vineyards and a couple of hills, then we flew over our house, circled it, then carried on up to the mountains. Past Faugères and its windmills, we turned left towards Lamalou-les-Bains where Alphonse Daudet used to soak and suffer. Past the nine-hole golf course and along the course of the river Orb. From here the views to the south and the north could not be more different. South to the sea is all vineyards and sun-soaked towns. North towards Paris it is all mountains and forests and big wheat fields. We looked down. There was Saint-Chinian. We managed to recognise the house of a friend, then we were high over Béziers and off to the coast. You could make out the tiny figures of people on the beach, walking their dogs and paddling. Along to Sète, which looked more appealing from the air, as there was no need to wait in an infernal traffic jam. Then over the Etang de Thau – no danger of running aground this time – over Pézenas and Saint Siméon and then back to Nizas and the solid ground.

There is a section of the coast that you only see as you motor down the Autoroute towards Spain. Nobody seems to go there much; we have been there in August and there has been nothing but a couple of people walking, flamingos, seagulls, wild thyme and lavender blowing in the wind. If the Scots had got here first they would have built a golf course, but instead it is just an empty corner. You cannot even hear the cars go by although occasionally you can catch sight of them. Not far away in Bages there is a restaurant called the Portanel. Here you can enjoy a fantastic view of the estuary while enjoying a dozen oysters, a bottle of La Clape, followed by eel from the lagoon.

La Clape is an intriguing place, certainly much more appealing than its name suggests. It used to be an island, cut off from the mainland in the days when the sea would lap against the cathedral in Narbonne. Now Narbonne is marooned, its cathedral sticking up in the plain like a ship that has run aground during low tide. La Clape acts as if it were still an island. Its winemakers are an independent bunch. The white wine contains a little-known grape called Bourboulenc. Like Picpoul, which is grown a bit further along the coast, it is dry, acidic and without much flavour or smell.

Sète was built at the mouth of the Canal du Midi, the melting pot where boats and traders would gather before goods were sent up river to Bordeaux and beyond. Sète is still a bustling port, probably France's busiest fishing town on the Mediterranean, although it has lost much of the business it had importing wine from Algeria. There are some great beaches to the west along the narrow spit of land that separates the sea from the Etang de Thau. There are numerous fish restaurants lining the main road, a bustling fish market, and many cafés that overlook the canal that runs through the centre of town. Jousting takes place on this canal during the summer months. Two boats, specially equipped for the event, carry about 20 men with oars and, out on a bowsprit, a man with a jousting pole. His job is to knock off his opponent on the opposition boat.

Up on the Mont St Clair, a limestone outcrop that overlooks the town, there is a chapel with a stunning view. The building itself is unremarkable, a plain small tower topped by a white Madonna. But the interior of Notre Dame de la Salette is quite special, even if most of the guide books ignore it. The walls have been painted in a deceptively simple style, the work owing much to painters such as Georges Braque, Picasso or even the comic books of Hergé. There are fish everywhere, swimming or cut up on a table, ready for lunch. Portraits of the 12 disciples are painted around the altar. Over the arches is a large Christ. On his left the sea is calm, the boats at anchor. On his right hand a storm is brewing and the boats are keeling over. Opposite Christ is a wall of 20th century figures, women in uniform, caps and badges, and my favourite, a Charlie Chan lookalike with little round glasses. It is the colour as well as the technique that makes the work so impressive. But there is no indication of the identity of the artist. We asked at the shop outside. No idea, the shop assistant said. Ask the priest. But we had a boat to catch.

Montségur, November 2001

Catharism comes from the East – a legate gets speared
– the buggering of cats – Raymond gets a whipping – a
bonfire in Béziers – Simon de Montfort's door – the
siege of Carcassonne – a one-eyed man leads the blind
from Bram – the religious dogs of war – the Cathars'
last stand – a bad lunch – sunset over Quéribus

*Y*OU WERE NEVER A Catholic were you? In fact, I
don't remember you being particularly religious at
all. You were probably the last generation that was
supposed to be religious. So what happened? Were you
taken to church and paid no attention? I remember you
told me you were educated at a convent. That was
probably enough to put you off. Hardly anyone seems to
be religious at all these days, with the exception of
Americans and au pairs, who all claim to be Buddhists.
Buddhism seems to be the most acceptable religion to
adopt, although down here it might be a bit cranky,
because there are so many insects and lizards that you
have to kill them before they bite you. It's you or them,
and frankly at midnight it's not an option. As for other

religions, they are too didactic for me. I remember you saying once when I was a child that you thought man created God, rather than the other way round. Even if it weren't an original thought, it struck me as quite profound.

The Languedoc is a good place to witness religion at its worst. It could make a saint agnostic. For we are not the first northern visitors. The history of the Languedoc is one of invasion, followed by persecution. Maybe it is because the Languedoc sounds like a banner flying in the wind that so many people have been tempted to attack it. The meaning of the word is less poetic than it sounds, describing just the division between the south, where yes is 'Oc' and the north, where yes is 'Oïl'. The most notorious and bloody attack took place nearly 800 years ago, when the Pope sent an envoy to visit the count of Toulouse. Languedoc then was a separate kingdom to France, split up between the fiefdoms of Toulouse, Béziers and the count of Aragon. The new Pope, Innocent III, was horrified at the spread of heresy in the Languedoc. Just how innocent was he? Not much. He could lay claim to one of the least apt names in history.

Early dissenters from the power of the Catholic Church had begun moving to the south, where they found a friendly, laissez-faire atmosphere. The count of Toulouse was only interested in sleeping with well-bred women: as a youth he seduced his father's mistress, committed incest with his sister, and married five times. He was happy to leave the running of his court to Jews and non-Catholics.

Many of these non-Catholics had been converted to Catharism – an heretical doctrine from the East, which had at its core a belief in dualism. Everything on earth was evil: hell was not in the afterlife, but here and now. Everything unseen, spiritual and evanescent, was good. The Devil was on earth; God was in heaven. The Eucharist, the basis of the Catholic Church, and the Pope's authority, was anathema to the Cathars. The Catholic bishops in Narbonne and Toulouse were renowned for their greed and love of drinking. They were obsessed by the material world. Food, wine, wealth, the colour of a carpet or the quality of a painting did not concern the Cathars. Only by abstaining from the material world could one attain spiritual heights. Smaller matters such as race, sex, nobility of birth did not matter. This encouraged a liberalism and lack of bigotry rather refreshing in an age of religious oppression. People could have sex before marriage if they chose; women could worship and even preach. When the Toulousian heretic, Peter Garcia, was interrogated by the Inquisition, he explained the position succinctly: 'God is perfect; nothing in the world is perfect; therefore God could not have created the world.'

This syllogism is reassuring for anyone who has asked how God can allow suffering in the world, but it did not reassure the Pope or his men. These fundamentalists were deeply disturbing to the ruling powers. The Pope agreed with Thomas Aquinas, who thought of heretics as coin counterfeiters. If the state could execute people for forging currency, should not the church be allowed to execute those who produce a counterfeit teaching of the church's thoughts? He sent his legate, Peter of Castelnau, to convince the Count of Toulouse that he should be ridding his land of these heretics, rather than just molesting his sister and her friends. Raymond VI's response was lukewarm. Next morning a lone knight approached the camp of the Papal envoy and ran him through with a spear, before galloping off into the mist. The culprit was never caught, but Raymond VI attracted the blame. Even if he could not be accused directly of the murder, it suited the Catholic Church and the local bishops to argue that he was somehow responsible.

Pope Innocent III called for a Holy War against the heretics, who, among other crimes, were accused of buggering cats. Anybody prepared to trek to the Languedoc to fight for just 40 days would be granted special Papal favours and ensured immediate entrance to Heaven. In a time of crusading, this beat a long journey to Palestine to face the infidels and God knows what else. Even though Philip Augustus, the king of France, was not initially keen on the concept of a civil war, this would turn out to be a convenient opportunity to unite his kingdom. He gave his barons leave to pursue the Pope's vendetta. A number of them, including Simon de Montfort, made the journey south to meet up with the Pope's army.

When Raymond VI realised the forces gathering against him, he made a cunning strategic move. Had he not fought with the crusaders against the infidel in the last crusade? He was no heretic. He rode to Aubenas to meet Abbot Arnauld-Amaury, leader of the Cistercian monks who had been put in charge of the crusade by the Pope, and begged for forgiveness. Arnauld-Amaury replied that as the Pope had excommunicated Raymond, only he could lift the order. After appeals to the Pope, he met with three archbishops and 19 bishops at St-Gilles cathedral. Stripped to the waist, Raymond swore to obey the instructions of the church, promised to give up land, control of some of his castles, apologised for encouraging Jews and heretics, assaulting bishops, and protecting the murderer of Peter of Castelnau. Then a stole was passed around his neck and he was led up to the altar, all the while being beaten by a whip.

Humiliating, but not life threatening. I know people working in the City of London who would pay handsomely for such an experience. Raymond emerged from the cathedral with most of his land intact, if not his dignity. Raymond now joined the crusader army. By becoming one of the aggressors, he could limit the threat to his kingdom. In addition, he could settle a few scores with his nephew, Raymond-Roger Trencavel, viscount of Béziers and his greatest enemy. They loathed each other with all the enmity that only family members can show each other, brought about by years of feuding over boundaries and Raymond-Roger's obvious disdain for his uncle's louche behaviour. The crusading army hurried on to Béziers. Raymond-Roger of Trencavel, Lord of Béziers and Carcassonne, had met with the leaders of the Crusade in Montpellier and sued for peace. He was not a Cathar, he said, but was powerless to stop the heretics from living in his lands. His argument did not persuade Arnauld-Amaury, who refused to listen to his excuses. Raymond-Roger hurried to Béziers to warn them of the threat, then continued on to Carcassonne, a more suitable site to repel an invading force. He took with him the entire Jewish community of the city. They were deemed too valuable to leave behind. The Jews in turn were happy to get out of the path of the crusaders. They still had unhappy memories of the crusade against the Spanish Moors in 1065, when Jews were killed indiscriminately.

As the army passed through southern France, it followed the same pattern, killing any Jews it came across. A few days later on July 22, the citizens of Béziers woke up to find their bishop, who had been with the crusading army, entering the city on a mule. At a public meeting in the cathedral he warned the people of the strength of the gathered army. He had with him a list of 200 known heretics. 'Give up these people,' he said, 'and the city will be spared.' As he spoke the army of Arnauld-Amaury began setting up its camp to the south of the city, on the other side of the river Orb. From their vantage point on the citadel, where the cathedral stands overlooking the river Orb, the people watched as the tents were pitched.

There is still a good view from the cathedral today. You look down on the river about 200 metres below, across at the bridges, then westward toward the plain that runs all the way to Carcassonne. The view may not have changed, but the cathedral has. The citizens of Béziers listened to what the bishop had to say, but rejected his plan. They figured that they were strong enough to resist the invaders. They had plenty of food and water. If they could hold out for a month the crusaders would run short of food and patience. Help might also come from Raymond-Roger, or the Count of Aragon, Peter II. The bishop, realising that he was losing the argument, left hurriedly with a few locals who felt they were safer outside the walls of Béziers.

Soon afterwards, and quite unexpectedly, hostilities began. Historians are divided on the reasons for the sudden attack. Some blame the death of a crusader who was bathing in the river when he was ambushed by the citizens and killed. His comrades stormed the city in revenge. The knights, seeing their men attacking the walls, followed suit. Within hours the people of Béziers were under attack, unprepared and without the stomach to withstand a siege.

What followed was an act of almost unprecedented inhumanity, as shocking as any atrocity during the Holocaust. Leading the mob was Arnauld-Amaury. When asked how they should distinguish Catholics from heretics, he is said to have replied: 'Kill them all. God will know his own.' He did little to stop the indiscriminate killing, nor did he show any remorse afterwards. Because they would not hand over 200 suspected heretics, men, women, priests, children, dogs and babies were all slaughtered. Although the Cathédrale St-Nazaire is the biggest religious building in Béziers and was rebuilt in 1215, it wasn't where the worst of the killing took place. This was slightly across town, near where the market stands today. The townspeople huddled in the Church of la Madeleine, but it did them no good. They had taken refuge in the cathedral, seeking sanctuary in the one place in medieval times where it was safe to hide. But Arnauld-Amaury's butchers showed no mercy. First they attacked the citizens in their hiding place. Then as the army moved through the city, it set fire to the buildings. The fire spread to the churches and the cathedral, causing the high vault to collapse and provide a flaming mausoleum for the bodies huddled inside. It was only when the heat and smoke grew too oppressive later in the day that the army retreated to its camp to watch the city burn.

The Cathédrale St-Nazaire has been rebuilt to look more like a castle or stronghold, with narrow slits for windows and castellations. There is no mention of the atrocities that took place there. History has been airbrushed by the Catholic Church. But the cathedral must have towered above the remains of the city. It has high ceilings and an altar that looks like it has been made of plaster of Paris. For less than half a euro you can buy a history of the cathedral. It is a master of doublespeak. 'Destroyed by fire in 1209 the Cathedral was reconstructed in French Gothic architectural style, a style introduced by the barons of the north. This reconstruction marked the end of the Roman style cherished by the southerners.' There is no mention that the fire was started by the Catholics; nor that the church became a mausoleum. But people still remember.

Not many doors away from the castle is a château. From the outside it looks like offices or empty apartments, but press on a buzzer and you are admitted into a glorious courtyard. One afternoon I visited the house. An 83-year old widower lives alone in the property. He has been trying to sell it for three years with no success. If it were in London or New York it would be worth £10 million. But in Béziers, a city that time has forgotten, he cannot get more than £500,000 for the place. It's a pity, because it is magnificent. There are wooden and tiled floors, large drawing rooms, and a kitchen that looks like it was designed more than 50 years ago. It is spotlessly clean. It was early evening when we visited. There is a note on the kitchen table telling the cook what the owner wants for dinner. In the dining room the table has been laid for one. There is a half bottle of wine from the Abbaye de Valmagne. The owner eats alone, because his wife died a few years earlier. There are many paintings of her on the walls. She was very beautiful. The owner says he wants to sell the place but he acts as if it were a shrine dedicated to her memory. He has an office and a workshop in the château, one of the most splendid workshops I have ever seen, with an elaborate mosaic for the tools, each saw in the right place, each tool's position marked by a white silhouette. He is an inventor and engineer. We are shown an intricate heating and generating system, obviously designed to kick in if the electricity supply ever fails. The place could withstand a siege. Outside in the terraced garden, there are views over the neighbouring land, down to where Simon de Montfort and his men camped. As we are leaving, the owner rustles in a drawer and pulls out a print. It shows the army of Simon de Montfort breaking through the walls of Béziers. The doorway through which they are entering Béziers is in his garden.

'This is the door that Simon de Montfort came through,' he says.

We go outside to have another look at it. It is barred now to keep out petty thieves and burglars. The sun shines on the walls. There is the sound of the fountain and far away, the noise of the traffic from the road. Despite the heat, the owner is wearing a three-piece black suit and a tie. He offers us a drink before we leave, but we are running late.

Carcassonne. There are some people who are mad about Carcassonne and one can understand why, even if one cannot share their enthusiasm. It reminds me of a toytown. All it lacks is lead soldiers. In *The Good Soldier*, Ford Madox Ford wrote: 'He wanted to marry her like some people want to go to Carcassonne.' Arnauld-Amaury wanted to go to Carcassonne, not to marry, but to murder. News of the slaughter at Béziers had spread through the countryside. Envoys from neighbouring cities such as Narbonne hurried to pay homage to the crusaders. They promised food and drink and to deliver them all known heretics. Villagers deserted their houses, many hurrying as refugees to Carcassonne. The army arrived not long behind them on the evening of July 28, just as the bells were being rung for vespers. If anywhere in the Languedoc could withstand a long siege, this was surely the place. The citadel is built on a steep slope. Twenty-six towers guard the walls. There was only one weakness, but it would prove to be a fatal one: the water supply. The castle is in sight of the river, but it could not draw any water from it. It had to rely on wells sunk within the walls. This might have been enough to satisfy the thirst of a small defending army, but the garrison had been swelled by all the fleeing villagers who had taken refuge in its walls.

The bulk of the army arrived on August 1 and set up camp by the side of the river. The next few days saw a couple of sorties, a small fight over the suburbs of St-Bourg, which saw the defenders driven back to the walls of the citadel and away from their last access point to the water. The crusaders brought in scaling ladders, mined the walls, but failed to make any lasting impact on the castle. With the fighting at an apparent stalemate, the attackers retreated to their camp, to feast and wait for something to happen. Unknown to them, something had already happened. The wells had run dry inside the city and disease was spreading among the people. Then a hope of salvation appeared in the guise of Peter II. The count of Aragon had a complex relationship with both Raymond-Roger Trencavel and Raymond VI, count of Toulouse. Nominally, the lands between Béziers and Carcassonne were suzerain to Peter II, by a complex series of marriage alliances and feudal allegiance. He rode into the crusaders' camp and offered to parley terms for a surrender. But Arnauld-Amaury was in no mood for a compromise. His offer was to let Raymond-Roger free, together with 11 companions and as many goods and possessions as they could carry. Not surprisingly, this offer was rejected. Peter returned to Aragon, leaving Carcassonne to its fate.

Despite the bleak conditions in the castle, the crusaders could make no impact. New terms were offered. The garrison would be spared, provided they walked out of the city in just their shirts and breeches. Raymond-Roger, together with nine of his men, accepted a safe conduct to negotiate in the tent of the count of Nevers. As a young man of 24 he may have believed in the notion of chivalry. It must have been a disheartening moment when he was seized and together with his men, cast into chains. He died just three months later, supposedly of dysentery, in his own dungeon deep below the walls of Carcassonne.

Out of the ruins of this battle emerged a new leader, Simon de Montfort, who would transform the Languedoc from a southern land with its own customs and traditions, to a province of France, under the control of the French king. Simon de Montfort was not the obvious choice to take control of the area after the defeat of Carcassonne. He had fought bravely and shown good leadership, but there were other knights with better credentials for the job. However, nobody else fancied it. Most knights felt they had fulfilled their obligations to the Pope and the King. They had secured their entry to the Kingdom of Heaven. Now they had to get back north, to their families and estates. In contrast, Simon de Montfort had nothing to lose. He had only a small estate in the Ile-de-France, the area around Paris, not enough for his ambition and certainly not enough for his large family. Despite being in his mid-40s, his soldiers were in awe of his energy and strength. He had a shock of red hair that made him recognisable even in the midst of the thickest fighting. He had rescued a soldier trapped in a ditch by the walls of Carcassonne, a brave thing to do when around him troops were retreating and he was under fire. He was an honest and incorruptible man, who felt himself to be a soldier of God. He told a Cistercian monk who came to console him in a moment of danger: 'Do you think I am afraid? My work is the work of Christ and the entire Church is praying for me. We cannot be defeated.' He was also ruthless.

Like any civil war, the Albigensian Crusade was marked by moments of horror. There is a well in Lavaur in the Minervois. When the townspeople ambushed and killed some of de Montfort's men, he killed the count, Aimery of Montréal, and pushed his sister, Geralda, down a well. There she was stoned and left to drown. Imagine the flies, the stench that came from this cesspit. But recall also that in the Middle Ages water did not come from a tap. The well was the source of water, almost of life itself. Throwing bodies in a well is worse than an act of war; it is likely to poison all the inhabitants.

In another gruesome episode, Simon de Montfort ordered that the captured garrison of Bram have their eyes put out, all except one of them, who was allowed to keep one eye in order to lead the blind men to Cabaret, a lot less fun than its name suggests. The priest was found among the defenders. He was dragged through the streets by a horse, then hanged from the walls. I have never been to Bram, but there is a signpost for it on the main road to Toulouse and I can never pass it without a shudder.

Despite early successes the war dragged on. In June 1218, two years after the Lateran Council handed the Languedoc to Simon de Montfort, he was still fighting. Pope Innocent had declared that Toulouse should be his capital, but the townspeople felt differently. De Montfort demanded money and hostages. The inhabitants put up barricades. A long siege followed. To break the deadlock de Montfort ordered the construction of a siege engine, that would throw huge stones at the walls. The day that it was wheeled into place the Toulousians decided that their only hope was to attack the siege engine and set fire to it. Led at dawn by the hot-headed Roger Bernard of Foix, a group clambered over the walls, crossed the moats and began heading towards the infernal machine. De Montfort was interrupted during mass. Like Sir Francis Drake, who waited to finish his game of bowls before finishing off the Spanish, de Montfort insisted on taking the consecration before launching a counter attack. This attack was as successful as Drake's, for he managed to repel the townspeople. But his brother, Guy, took an arrow in the groin. Rushing to help him, Simon was hit in the head by a rock that smashed his eyes, teeth, jaw and brains. Killed, you could say, stone dead.

'The wolf is dead!' shouted the Toulousians. The city was saved. De Montfort was dead at the age of 53. His eldest son Amaury carried on the fight, but he had neither his father's cunning nor cruelty. Another son, Simon, went to England, where he became Earl of Leicester, launched a rebellion against the King, won the Battle of Lewes but was killed at the Battle of Evesham, where his body was disembowelled by royalist supporters. Even so, he is credited with being the catalyst for the first British Parliament in 1265.

Back in the Languedoc, a degree of religious tolerance

developed, until the papacy of Gregory XI in 1227. He unleashed the Dominicans, literally the Domini Canes – the dogs of the Lord. The Dominicans were founded by Saint Dominic, who set up a nunnery with the sole purpose of helping those who had renounced Catharism. By any standards they were an evil bunch, a Languedoc precursor of the East German Stasi, who controlled the population by fear and threats. They hunted in pairs and tore about the country, trapping people into confessing their Catharism. This was easier than it might appear, because Cathars were not allowed to swear oaths. Thus anybody who refused to vow their allegiance to Catholicism was denounced. They were then forced to convert to Catholicism or face death by burning. People were rewarded for betraying their neighbours. Some gave in quietly; others perished on bonfires.

Many of the Cathars, the supposedly peace-loving, vegetarian feminists, wanted nothing more than a quiet life. I suspect that they weren't all driven fanatics. Many of them were drawn to the Cathar Church in protest at the excesses of the Catholic Church – the rich landowning monks who controlled huge swathes of land, the corrupt bishops who sold entry into heaven like modern vendors of timeshare properties. The Cathar Church neither condemned usury nor demanded tithes. This earned it the support not only of religious fanatics, but also of city dwellers who just wanted a quiet life free from bills.

In a sense the Cathars are the forerunners of

Protestantism. Both were engaged in the textile industry of the region; both wanted neither help from the Church nor its taxes and demands. The Catholic Church managed to eradicate the Cathars in northern Italy and northern France. In England they were branded with hot irons. In southern France they were slaughtered. But their movement led to Luther and the Reformation and even more violent religious wars.

The Cathars' last stand was at the castle of Montségur. This is a seemingly impregnable fortress high in the hills beyond the Corbières in the foothills of the Pyrénées. To reach it you have to travel to Perpignan, then take the D117 and head inland. The first part of the journey takes you through wild bare country, whipped dry by the wind. This is the sweet wine country of Maury and its most famous product, Mas Amiel. We did not stop to sample the wine, but carried on, through a rocky gorge where there was just a river, a railway track up above and a road cut out of the rock. Often you were driving under a rocky overhang, so dark that it seemed that the sun never shone there. After about an hour's drive the road begins to climb, then you reach a plateau, where the fields look large and fertile. This is a land of wide open spaces, tall trees bent in the wind, and just a few villages. The houses have an alpine look: tall with small windows and high roofs to bear the weight of the snow.

After another hour's driving you reach Montségur. The first sight of it on its 'Pog' – the name given to the small hillock that sticks up like a thumb – is unforgettable. On the very top of the thumb, perched at an impossibly high angle, overlooking all the other hills and mountains, is the castle. As we got closer we saw the bare rock on the eastern side, then we hit snow. The tail end of the car began to twitch.

'This is the reason I got rid of my Jaguar,' said Peter.

We climbed and climbed, then the castle disappeared. We wondered if it had been a dream, then we came across the village of Montségur which crouches at the base of the hill and up above, the castle. It was now 12 o'clock. This is the witching hour for French people. Unfortified by their meagre croissants, this is the time of day when they need food. We thought it would be worthwhile to make sure we could have lunch somewhere after we had made the climb to the top, so we stopped at the first restaurant we could find. We discovered afterwards that it was also the only restaurant that was open. The owner told us that we could have lunch if we were there before 13.15. He put another log on the fire and told us that when that burnt out, lunch would be over.

'Are you planning to climb up?' he asked.

'Yes,' I said.

'In those shoes?' he demanded, pointing at my tennis shoes.

'Yes.' He looked unhappy.

'It is hyper-dangerous,' he said. 'I would not go up if I were you. You might be able to get up, but to get down, that is another matter. You could easily fall and break your leg or ankle. Hyper, hyper-dangerous.'

But he had not been driving since eight o'clock that morning to get there. Nor did he understand that the English are the heirs of George Leigh Mallory and Francis Whymper, who invented climbing in the Alps armed with only a bar of Kendal mint cake and a tweed jacket. Surely a short walk up a path to a castle could not be dangerous.

'Good luck,' he said, looking at me as if for the last time, as if I were setting off up the Matterhorn. Maybe it was just that he thought he was about to lose a precious customer, but I found his concern touching.

'Don't be late for lunch,' he added, as we turned to leave.

The car slithered further up the hill, then we parked and began walking across a snow-covered field. Peter was wearing deck shoes, which slipped beneath him. Stephanie, a writer friend, had chosen wisely, her Nike Air trainers carrying her up through the snow with the grip of a husky. But she was weighed down by an enormous camera. It soon became clear that neither she nor Peter would be accompanying me to the top.

'You go on,' said Peter. 'Leave us behind.'

'Take my camera,' said Stephanie.

So, armed with the camera, I trudged up through the snow and into the trees. The going was not too bad and I was making good time until I was stopped by a man sitting in a small hut.

'Three euros, twenty centimes,' he said.

Taxed by an authority as iniquitous as the Catholic Church, I continued up the rocks and steps. I admired the French attitude to danger, here and at subsequent castles. They do not rope everything off. If you are fool enough to go climbing somewhere that you might fall and hurt yourself, that is up to you. They won't ruin it for everybody else by interfering with the scenery.

As I climbed up through the snow, I passed a small sign that told me that this was a medieval path. Here it said were the hoofmarks of medieval asses. I couldn't see any of the marks, but assume they were covered with snow. By now the view was outstanding. I stopped for a moment to catch my breath. It was surprisingly hot work. Even though there was a keen breeze, I was sweating under my collection of jumpers and jackets. I looked towards the sun and the snow fields of the Pyrénées. High up the path were the forbidding walls of the castle.

The Cathars had persuaded Raymond de Pereille, the local landowner, to build them a castle at the beginning of the 13th century, about the time that their soulmates were being savaged in Béziers and Carcassonne. They didn't live in the castle, but in the village below. The idea of the castle was a lookout and a place to shelter in times of trouble. There was to be plenty of that.

Even though Montségur is a long drive in a Jaguar and an even longer march on a battle-horse, the crusaders could not keep away. As part of his penance Raymond VII, the count of Toulouse, sent a force to besiege the castle in 1224. It was by all accounts a half-hearted effort. A later army set out in earnest. The Cathars had only themselves to blame. They had been largely ignored by the authorities, but one night in 1242 they sent a small force of soldiers to Avignonet, a small town near Toulouse. Contrary to their supposedly peace-loving, vegetarian nature, they broke into the lodgings of two Dominicans, and killed them.

The Pope was out for revenge. He sent Hugh d'Acis, a French knight who was the king's man in Carcassonne, to smoke them out of their mountain lair. In May 1243 he and a couple of thousand men advanced towards the castle. Inside were 200 men, led by Pierre-Roger of Mirepoix. All summer and autumn they surrounded the castle as best they could, but it is not an easy place to surround. Supplies and men were still getting in. In November help came from the bishop of Albi, who was also something of a military engineer. He set up a trebuchet on a steep slope near the castle and began pounding the men inside with rocks and stones. Pierre-Roger withdrew his men from the eastern part of the castle to save them from danger, but also in the belief that the steep cliff would be sufficient to deter any invaders. He was wrong. On a moonless night in January 1244, a group of Basques scaled the rocks and managed to establish a foothold in the eastern wing of the castle. It is said that when they looked down the next morning, they were horrified by what they had climbed. Even so, attempts to dislodge them failed. It was enough to persuade the inhabitants of the castle that the game was up. On March 2 1244, Pierre-Roger and his men surrendered.

There is a small wooden balcony with a staircase that is the entry to the castle. I went in. There was nothing there, except some footprints in the snow. The wind howled through the entrance opposite. There is not much left standing, just four walls and an empty sky above. On the far wall there was an icy staircase, the rail of which disappeared half-way up. But to get a decent photo of the view I knew I would have to go up the stairs.

I strapped the camera over my shoulder and began the slow climb. What if I slipped? Peter would never get up here in his boating shoes and Stephanie would be more worried about her camera. We would also miss lunch… But I forced myself up, a step at a time, until the world opened below me: north to Toulouse, east to Perpignan and the Mediterranean Sea, and south to Spain. It is hard to imagine a view that has changed less in 800 years. There are trees, valleys, hills, but no towns or motorways or large industrial buildings. It is easy to picture a look-out on these walls spotting an approaching army. I went back down the slithering staircase and through a small doorway. The path was thick with snow and there were no footsteps. Conscious of the need to hurry or go hungry, I walked along the path that led to a small terrace. It was sheltered from the wind. Here would be a grand place for a picnic, watching the eagles wheeling below. I made a snowball and threw it at an imaginary invader, then retreated.

When the garrison of Montségur came down the slope, it was to a mixed reception. Those who were willing to swear an oath of allegiance to the Church were allowed to go free. But for the committed Cathars there was to be no mercy. They were chained together and led down the hill. There a bonfire was waiting for them. Begged to recant or reconsider their beliefs, they refused. More than 200 Cathars died in a crackling few minutes, including Bertrand de Marty, the last bishop to preside over the Cathar communities of the region.

Pierre-Roger and his men were allowed one more night in the castle. What happened during this night has been the subject of much speculation. A few weeks earlier, the castle's treasure trove, said to contain gold, silver and a great deal of money, had been hidden in a cave. Three Cathars, who had been hidden in his living quarters, were dispatched down the cliff to rescue the treasure. The next day Pierre-Roger and his men walked down from the castle, made their excuses, and left. But was that treasure really the lost ark of the covenant? What happened to Pierre-Roger? History does not relate, but that has not stopped people asking the question nor making up their own fanciful explanations, such as the possibility that it may even have contained the Holy Grail.

Hurrying down, but conscious of the danger of the steps, we made it back to the restaurant before the log on the fire had died out. We were the only people in the place. The food was ordinary; the wine worse. The proprietor told us that he knew very little about running a restaurant, but had moved from the north of France in search of a small hotel. When the deal fell through, he and his wife acquired the restaurant. He complained that he could only make money in the tourist season. The rest of the year he might as well close, he said. The locals won't come. Our sympathy was with the locals.

An hour's drive away, the splendidly named Château de Peyrepertuse is even more gravity-defying than its name suggests. In fact, although I have never visited Krak des Chevaliers nor a hundred other castles, I suggest that this is the best castle in the world to visit. It has everything you would want in a castle except a maiden in the tower and a madman in the dungeon. But the building on the top of a steep hill is audacious and brilliant. It is bigger than Montségur and authentic. I only learnt on the journey from castle to castle that the walls I had been clambering on were not Cathar walls. They were built later, after the original walls had been destroyed. In general I am not in favour of rebuilding: I am still reeling from the shock that the Pont du Gard is not original. This is the aqueduct that linked Nîmes to its water supply up in the hills above Uzès. Its heroic proportions were shattered by an earthquake, and its stone plundered by local monks when they wanted to build churches. It was left to Napoleon III to show us the grandeur of the Roman Empire. Pretty grand it is too, but the second most visited monument in France is only 200 years old, not 2,000 as they pretend. Even so, it is worth a visit, although you have to remember that the stones you are seeing were not put there by men in togas.

Peyrepeteuse has been rebuilt and added to over the years, but with a view to strengthening the fortifications, not creating a tourist attraction. Once the Cathar threat had been destroyed the castle retained a defensive role as one of the most southern castles defending France from Spain. It perches on top of a row of steep limestone rock, so that at first it looks like a part of the rockface itself. It is almost as if it fell from the sky, landing as if by chance on the vertiginous cliffs. As you get nearer you can make out the walls, but first you have to wind up the road to the car park, then head down a path that skirts round the back of the castle, then climbs up again to the main entrance. There are two main parts to the castle. From the very top, there is a chapel called San Jordi. Up here the wind blows even on the calmest day. We watched the shadow of the castle stalk across the hill opposite, then looked in the other direction to the Mediterranean, where we could just make out the silhouette of the last castle we were planning to visit, Castle Quéribus.

Quéribus was the last stronghold of the Cathars, before they dispersed to the hills and valleys of the Pyrénées and

Spain. They stayed on at Quéribus for another 10 years, until King Louis XI's men captured Chabert de Barbaira, the local lord who was a Cathar sympathiser. He was forced to hand over the castle in exchange for his freedom. The Cathars slipped away into the night, settling for a life of hidden rituals. The Catholic church had won. Their hegemony would last another 200 years, until a fresh wave of reformation swept through Europe under the leadership of Martin Luther.

We got to Quéribus at six o'clock. The ticket office was closed, so there would be no money to pay. I looked up at the path that leads up to the castle. There was probably only another half an hour of daylight left and it might take that just to get to the top. I decided against running up the hill. Two Cathars castles in a day are enough for anybody. We walked around the car park where two hippy-looking men were talking earnestly. This looked as good a place as any to conclude a drug deal. There was just one cloud in the sky, shaped like an inverted pyramid. We watched it turn pink, then black, then got in the Jaguar and headed back down the road to the coast.

Antidote Bar, Montpellier, May 2003

The mayor of Montpellier – how to
rejuvenate a city – a team of architects –
moving to the sea – a glass of whisky – a
heatwave – old men in loud clothing – a
race up Fontfroide – Lilliane's legs

T IS A WARM, balmy evening and I am sitting in the Antidote Bar in the Place de la Canourge in Montpellier, looking at the girls and the paintings on the wall. They are by an artist called Roland Lamon. They are painted on cardboard, sometimes three or four different layers, as if to give a sense of perspective. He paints beach scenes, naked girls watched by plump men in shorts and glasses, sailing boats and lighthouses. I rather like the paintings. I ask the barman how much they are, but he says that he has not yet been given the prices.

I like sitting here. I have spent the last couple of days wandering around the city. There is no doubt it has changed enormously. If you were a resident of Montpellier who by some misfortune had spent the last 20 years either in a coma or the French Foreign Legion, you would return to familiar but much changed surroundings. You would recognise the old town with its cathedral, Jardin des Plantes and university buildings, but the cars that used to clog the narrow streets have all gone underground. As you walk down to the Place de la Comédie, dodging out of the way of the new blue tram decorated with white swallows, you would notice that the old parade ground has been turned into a housing and office centre called Antigone; past the Musée Fabre, an opera house has been built; there is a new library, swimming baths, the river Lez has become a canal which leads to a harbour, while on the outskirts of the city there is an enormous leisure, housing and shopping complex under construction. What, you might ask yourself, has been going on? Who is responsible for this?

The answer lies in one of the most unprepossessing quarters of Montpellier at the Hôtel de Ville. In his fifth floor office Georges Frêche, mayor of Montpellier since 1977, is holding endless meetings with planners, businessmen and journalists. You might expect to meet a small, hyperactive megalomaniac, but instead Frêche is tall, slightly overweight, and bears all the legacies of the years he spent as a second row rugby forward playing in Toulouse, in the days when a second row forward lumbered around the field, socks around his ankles and knees covered in mud, rarely touching the ball. When he walks he moves with a sway, because his back is injured from too many scrums. His office is large, but elegantly decorated, with light olive-green curtains, a glass desk, a handball trophy and a statue of a man and a dog. There is no computer and very little paperwork.

He may be slow on his feet, but he is a hard man to pin down for an answer as to how he has transformed Montpellier. Everyone agrees that he and his energetic administration have changed a sleepy, sunburnt city, living off a dwindling reputation for producing table wine and heavy-drinking doctors, into a first-class place to live and work. No European city can match the growth of Montpellier in the last 30 years. Unlike many French towns and cities, where the clock seems to have stopped some time during the reign of Napoleon III, Montpellier has undergone a stunning renaissance. From being France's twenty-fifth city, it is now seventh, overtaking Bordeaux on the way. The population has risen from 20,000 in 1962 to around 200,000 now. New businesses have been encouraged to set up offices in the technology parks. Students flock to study in Montpellier, attracted by the courses and the climate. Many are so beautiful they could be on a sabbatical from their modelling agencies. The world's top architects have helped transform the landscape, excited by the vision of Frêche and his deputy, Raymond Dugrand. As the American architect Richard Meier said when he first arrived from New York: 'I realised that the city had a vision of itself, that something important was happening here, and I wanted to be part of it.'

The man responsible for this vision is more interested in talking about the economic threat that China poses in the 21st century, America's economic hegemony in the 20th century, and how Japan is now a spent force in Asia. He admires the Americans for their fighting spirit, noting that Europe is possibly too civilised. 'We are like Rome in the third century,' he says.

But he has managed to keep the barbarians from the gates, partly by integrating them into his civilised city. So how did he manage to perform the most spectacular transformation of a European city in the last 20 years? 'How did we do it?' he asks. 'Because I had the desire to do it.'

Frêche grew up near Toulouse, where he was one of the brightest students of his generation. His studies took him to Paris at the tail end of the 1960s, where as a Marxist he was caught up in the excitement of 1968. He became a law teacher, first in Bordeaux, then Montpellier. After a brief spell working with the Minister of Finance ('a man from the right with whom I had nothing in common'), he ran for mayor of Montpellier, but retained his position at the university. He still teaches. Students of the industrial revolution from 1700–1914 and the history of political thought, including the works of Plato and Aristotle, may be surprised to find that it is the mayor of the city who is marking their papers. It is perhaps this grasp of economic history that has helped him attract new investment to the city.

'I could see in the 1970s that the future for this city lay in its intellect,' he says. 'I saw what was going on in America, with Silicon Valley, the development around Boston and other areas, and thought that we could do the same thing here.' He was helped by a number of factors: Montpellier had no existing industrial base, so there was nothing to lose by changing direction; it did have a strong university base, so there was a well-educated workforce who could be retrained; and in 1962, IBM had decided to make Montpellier its headquarters in France. IBM's arrival in the city inspired other firms to follow, such as Dell. They would help provide some of the money and attract the people to realise Frêche's ambitious plans. The final trend in Frêche's favour was the natural movement of people from the north of France to the south, in search of sunshine and a better way of living. This echoed what happened in America a decade earlier, when natives of Chicago and Detroit moved to Florida and California.

'The fact remains that Montpellier's city charter, put to its populace in 1977, and endorsed at a time when nobody else in France dared to speak of projects and planning, is still the basis for its renaissance,' says Raymond Dugrand, head of Urban Planning and Public Works. He is a technocrat, a small serious man with grey hair and a grey suit, whose job it is to turn Frêche's vision into reality. He cannot talk without taking out a pencil and sketching a plan of how the city has developed, and how it will continue to develop. The aim was conceived to turn Montpellier into a Eurocity, with world-class skills based in science and technology parks. It has been developed with single-minded persistence.

French mayors are among the most powerful rulers of cities in the world, matched only by their counterparts in Germany and the United States. Despite France's centralisation, they are capable of exerting enormous influence on their cities. In some instances, notably in Nice, this power has been misused, and the mayor impeached. Frêche seems to have escaped any accusation of corruption. To help achieve his vision, he has used his influence with his socialist colleagues in Paris to help benefit his constituents. His friendship with Jack Lang is credited with helping him obtain the loans he needed. His critics say that Paris only gave him what he wanted in order to get rid of him. He insists that he tries to work with Paris at all times. 'My motto is, if it is possible, to work with Paris. If not, without Paris. But never against Paris.'

A grand plan was conceived to give Montpellier a complete makeover. Old buildings were renovated; new areas were developed. This was done as a public and private partnership, but in a controlled manner, unlike the development in areas such as London's Docklands, where the infrastructure was the last thing to be put in place. The tram already runs to the new Odysseum complex, even though the area has yet to be finished. 'I can't trust the market to organise the town,' says Dugrand. The mayor buys the land – by force if it has to, but according to Dugrand this right has never been exercised – then hands it over to the Société Mixte. This body then develops the area.

Over the last 20 years Montpellier has used the cream of modern architects, including Ricardo Bofill, Christian de Portzamparc, Adrien Fainsilber, Paul Chemetov and Claude Vasconi. This revolutionary idea of using foreign architects in international competitions – only now being copied by cities such as London, Paris and Bilbao – has contributed to the quality of the buildings in the city. Architects are given a quarter to develop, the design of which must be approved by the mayor's office. There are four quarters under construction at present, with each quarter consisting of 12,000 homes. The design of these buildings is allowed to get more radical the further the buildings are from the centre of the city. Dugrand was keen to mix business and living areas and not to create modern ghettos far from the centre.

Antigone was the first major new development, which is just a short stroll from the Place de la Comédie. The architecture of Ricardo Bofill has been accused of fascism: the neo-classical design can be a bit daunting, but on a sunny day the buildings light up and children play in the squares. The mayor's team does not mind being ruthless. When it was realised that Antigone had no natural opening from the old city, an entire apartment block was demolished to make one. To this day the mayor is buying up every second apartment block in the suburbs and blowing it up. 'The fundamental rule is the right to beauty,' says Dugrand. 'For those who live in the outer suburbs as well as in the city centre, for inhabitants of private houses as well as social housing.'

Frêche and his team have fought hard to try to avoid creating ghettos based on either race or wealth. In every quarter there is an element of social housing. This was a unique proposition in France at the time, even though it has now been copied. Frêche's vision has remained loyal to his socialist roots. On the walls of his outer office are photos of his heroes: de Gaulle (before he became president); Jean Jaurès (a socialist minister); Chile's Allende; and Léon Blum, the first Jewish prime minister of France in the 1930s and leader of the socialist party. Léon Blum is also a stop on the tram, proof perhaps that the mayor's influence is ubiquitous in the city.

At one time, Frêche intended to use Montpellier as a stepping stone for greater things in Paris, but personal differences with Mitterand kept him out of office. Paris's loss is Montpellier's gain. He is not short of new ideas for the city. Not content with building a new port complex, Port Marianne, and a multiplex area, Odysseum, Frêche quickly sketches out his plans for the next 12 years. He wants to build a contemporary arts centre ('like the Guggenheim in Bilbao only more beautiful'), and move the Hôtel de Ville to Port Marianne.

Critics who try to point out that he is spending money that he cannot afford are rebuffed when he explains that the public money in the Odysseum is only eight per cent of the total cost, with the private sector making up the difference. 'Within three years the city will have no debt,' says Frêche. He is not repaying the debt by squeezing his passengers, for a day pass on the tram only costs 3.5 euros.

Frêche now wants to attract genetic and green technology companies, believing that this will be a source of growth in the next 20 years. It is perhaps this long-range vision, coupled with the mandate that the Montpellierains have given him, which sets him apart from other mayors and town planners in Europe. He has been confident of having enough time to finish his task, unlike London's Ken Livingstone perhaps, who is so keen to make a mark that he has conceived a grand plan to kill all the city's pigeons.

Frêche is also the author of a number of economic studies, including the snappily titled *Les prix des grains, des vins et des légumes à Toulouse 1486–1868*. But he is no stern technocrat or bean counter. He is passionately interested in sport and the arts, realising early on that establishing these cultural activities was essential for the success of the city. Nor is he a slave to artistic temperament. When he hired Jean-Paul Montanari, the energetic director of dance in Montpellier, he sat him down and taught him how to do a budget, so that Montanari would be in control of his own finances. Montanari shakes his head in admiration. 'What has happened in the city in the last 20 years has been a miracle,' he says. 'You know we have 40 dance companies here?'

Frêche does not seem to think of it as a miracle, but as something that happened because he wanted it to happen. His hero is the stoic Roman emperor Marcus Aurelius, and he lives by his motto: 'It is necessary to live each day in peace with oneself in order to be able to die with a smile on one's lips.' He is like the irritating bright person in the class, who finds calculus so easy that they finish the exam before most people have started and cannot understand what all the fuss is about. One day he might sit back and take pride in his achievements and spend more time with his five daughters, proof perhaps that you cannot dictate everything in life. But for the moment he is busy with the next project, taking Montpellier back to the sea. Unlike King Canute, who gave up because he could not control the waves, Frêche has decided that while you may not be able to rule the Mediterranean, you can at least control the shoreline.

'Montpellier is only 3.6 kilometres from the sea,' he says. 'When it was a medieval city, it was on the sea. Our ambition is to take it back towards the sea, rather as Barcelona did in the run-up to the 1992 Olympics. This will involve building a second tram line, more houses, parks and office buildings.'

A week after interviewing Frêche, I caught a plane from Montpellier airport to Paris. Sitting next to me was a local businessman.

'How did you find Frêche?' he asked.

'Very interesting.'

'He rules the city like a medieval monarch. It is said that you can get him to do anything you want after two glasses of whisky.'

'How do you get him to drink the whisky?'

'That is the problem.'

We are in the middle of a heatwave. It sneaked up on us one morning. The day got hotter and hotter until we grew faint and had to lie down after lunch. When we got up it had not gone away. Just moving a short distance became a chore. Every time you did anything, it was like being hit around the head by a warm frying pan. You seek the shade, but it is remorseless. The noise of the insects – the frantic screech of the cicadas – makes it worse. This has gone on now for nearly 20 days. It only gets cool briefly in the early morning, around five o'clock. During the day one longs for a cloud, or better, a rainstorm. But there is nothing. All the fans in the house are turning, the shutters closed against the sun, but it makes no difference. When you lie in bed you can feel drips of sweat trickling over your body. One longs to lie in an ice bucket like a bottle of rosé wine.

Not the best time, you might think, to take up cycling. For the past few years I have looked on amused at the sight of middle-aged men pedalling around the Hérault, bodies squeezed into too-tight lycra in ridiculous colours, bright purples, yellows and greens. Sunday morning is when you see them out in force. In England, men play golf on Sunday mornings. In France they go cycling. How absurd, I thought, how undignified. And then I was persuaded by a nice Englishman called John to join him and some of his French friends on a ride. As I felt in danger of doing no exercise, I acquired a bike and some padded shorts. Bikes have probably changed out of all recognition since your day. Do you remember that poem we learnt together for a recital competition when I was 11?

With lifted feet, hands still
I am poised, and down the hill dart
With heedful mind;
The air goes by in a wind.

Swifter and yet more swift,
Till the heart with a mighty lift
Makes the lungs laugh, the throat cry
O Bird, see, see bird I fly.

'Is this, is this your joy?
O bird, then I, though a boy,
For a golden moment share
Your feathery life in air!'

Say, heart, is there aught like this
In a world that is full of bliss!

'Tis more than skating, bound
Steel-shod to the level ground.

Speed slackens now, I float
Awhile in my airy boat;
Till, when the wheels scarce crawl
My feet to the treadles fall.
Alas, that the longest hill
Must end in a vale; but still,
Who climbs with toil, whereso'er
Shall find wings waiting there.

Going down Hill on a Bicycle was written by Henry Charles Beeching, a minor Victorian poet and clergyman. Was he, I wonder, any relation of the Beeching who cut all the rural railways? There would be an irony there – let them ride bikes, he might have said. Anyway, the unexpected choice – we found it in the *Oxford Book of English Verse*, but I am sure that subsequent editions have chucked him out in favour of some rap poet – was enough to win me third prize. I still recite parts of it as we head down hills, but now one's feet are strapped to the 'treadles' with clips. The first time I rode the bike I forgot about this and stopped. Unable to put my foot down, the bike and I capsized on the road. A better thing to witness, perhaps, than to experience. Luckily there was nobody watching, but I had the bruises for several days.

The Frenchmen we ride with are mainly retired.

Christian and Gérard used to work for the SNCF, the railways. Claude was a detective. Georges, the oldest at 70, worked for Renault. He wears the most garish clothing of all, partly I suspect, because he thinks it makes him attractive to women. Wherever we stop he is keen to start chatting to the local girls. He nearly crashed into a car the other day because he was staring so hard at a poster of a girl in a bikini. Later that day he was seen cycling off in the wrong direction after an English girl on a mountain bike. Sometimes Charlie, who was the butcher in Alignan-du-Vent for 40 years, joins us. Now in his late 60s, he is still extremely strong and fit. Once, returning from a long ride, he started performing acrobatics on his bike: standing on the seat, lying on the seat, riding it backwards. It would have been a remarkable sight if done by a monkey in a circus. Performed by a former butcher nearing 70, it was extraordinary.

We meet at the crossroads at Roujan at seven o'clock in the morning in the summer and eight o'clock in the winter, every Tuesday, Thursday and Sunday. Sometimes we ride for as much as five hours, covering over 100 kilometres. On Tuesdays we are met by Lilliane, who runs the toy shop in Pézenas. She is super-fit, having run the London marathon this year. She talks all the time, with only the toughest climbs reducing her to silence. Sometimes we stop for a coffee. Pierre will take a glass of red wine. He tells me stories of how he raced in the Paris-Brest-Paris, a cycling event that takes place once every two years. It is non-stop, nearly 1,200 kilometres long, and brutal. To train, he used to ride to the Costa Brava for the weekend, 300 kilometres there and 300 kilometres back.

It is the early mornings that I love best. On a still morning when nearly everyone else in the world is asleep, it is fun to ride through villages, smelling the bread from the bakery, passing the children reluctantly going to school, and overtaking the tractors heading to the vineyards. Sometimes Charlie sings Charles Trenet songs. We ride as a pack, wheels inches apart, until we come to a climb and then people get spread out. If it is a long climb the leaders will wait at the top, or head to the nearest water fountain to fill up the water bottles. Most villages have their own fountains: made of stone, with the date of manufacture carved proudly into the headpiece.

This last Sunday we covered more than 100 kilometres, riding through Neffies, up over a hill called la Roquette, a beautiful winding road that takes you up more than 300 metres so you have a view to the sea, down to Cabrières, on to Clermont l'Hérault and then north to St Jean de la Blaquière. It is different country here. There are olives, but no vines. The fields are bigger, growing wheat, and the air is cooler. Then a long six-kilometre climb up past a village called La Roquette, then a long sweeping descent down to Arboras, through St Saturnin and Jonquières, both wine towns, the fields surrounding them covered in vines. Skirting past Clermont l'Hérault, we stopped for water in Villeneuvette, a small town that had been dedicated to making woollen garments for the king. On the entrance is written 'Honneur au Travail'. There are splendid plane trees around the fountain that must be 250 years old. Back through Cabrières, up la Roquette from the other side, and then down to Neffies and into the bar in Roujan.

Hot and sweaty, we drank beer and shandy. Georges began to complain that all we do is go around looking at the countryside 'like cinema'. We are not treating it like a sport, he said.

'We should be doing competitions, cyclo club races,' he said. There was heated debate, then he asked me what I thought.

'I don't consider anything a sport unless there is a ball involved,' I said. 'Cricket, tennis, rugby, football. These are all sports. The rest is exercise.'

They shrugged this off, but I realised afterwards that this might have mightily offended them. For cyclists, it isn't just a sport, it is the sport, almost a way of life. What I see as an amusing way to see the countryside, as well as a good way of ensuring that I can still fit into a pair of trousers, they see it as something altogether more important. For a real cyclist, any time not spent on the bike is wasted. Their talk is of gears and brakes and tyre pressures. Their heroes are the great men who won the Tour de France, Jacques Anquetil, Laurent Fignon and Bernard Hinault. When they are not riding their bikes, they are cleaning them. Every time we pass through Pézenas we take a 10-minute pit stop at the bike shop.

They wander through, gazing in awe at the new machines and the accessories, as if they are in a church. I wait outside, watching the traffic.

As we got fitter, we went further. The biggest climb around here is the Col de Fontfroide, a 12-kilometre hour of pain and struggle. We set out at 6.45 one morning, the usual gaggle including Lilliane, even though it wasn't a Tuesday. She had never ridden up it before, but was in training for a duathlon. I had no idea what to expect, but I sensed that the mood was a bit more serious than usual.

We rode steadily up towards Faugères, the air cool and the light brilliant. The leaves on the vines shone a brilliant green, the only colour in a parched landscape. We passed a small temple, stuck by the side of the road. Then up through Faugères, past the petrol station that doubles as a wine shop, then on to the main Béziers to Bedarieux road. It is dual carriageway, with a nice new surface. This sort of thing is important to cyclists.

We swooped down the hill, under the railway bridge, then left before Herepian, where we joined a small road that joins the Orb. It is a little cooler here. The extra altitude, plus the presence of the river and the shade from the trees, is a relief from the wind and sun. Behind me Lilliane talks excitedly. Claude goes from person to person, looking around. Pierre cycles grimly, eyes focused, imagining perhaps that he is on the Paris-Brest-Paris and that there is still a long way to go.

We cross the Orb, then turn left to join the road to

Olargues and beyond. Everybody is keen to tell me that Olargues has been voted one of the loveliest villages in France. It's true that it has some nice buildings and a fine bridge, le Pont du Diable. But I have never managed to find anything very interesting in the place, so I did not mind that we pedalled past. After a couple more little hills, we reached the bottom of the Col, where we stopped for a drink and an energy bar. Claude pointed high up in the sky.

'That's where we are going,' he said. And he laughed.

I was quite eager to get going. If there is something awful to be done, I find the waiting around even more painful than the event. So I set off, in tandem with Claude and Gerard. As we began to climb we could hear Lilliane laughing behind us at one of Charlie's bad jokes. After a couple of corners I found that I wanted to go faster than the other two, so pulled away slightly.

'Don't go too fast,' said Claude. 'It's a long way.'

I waved my arm in recognition, but I was confident that I could keep going ahead of them. I gradually picked up the pace so that when I looked back before turning a corner, they were not even in sight. There are chestnut trees for shade on the lower portion, so I didn't feel too bad. If I could go faster than 12 kilometres per hour, I could make it up in less than an hour. Surely I could do that? I pushed the speed up to 15, 16 kilometres. There was no sound except my breathing and the whirr of the chain. A bead of sweat ran down my nose. I picked up my water bottle for a drink.

After a while you pass a small turning for a village, but you keep climbing. Suddenly, in this middle section, I found my pace slowing. Back to 13, now down to 12. If I keep this up I can still do it in an hour, I thought. But I looked at the verge. How pleasant it would be to prop the bike against a tree and lie in the shade. I forced myself on.

As you get out of the tree line, you begin to see what lies ahead of you. It is daunting. I stopped looking up. If I could just keep pedalling, then sooner or later I would reach that corner. It seemed less torturous than forcing yourself to watch something appear so slowly. My pace now was down to 11, sometimes as low as 10. At what point would I grind to a halt and topple over?

Suddenly I heard a dreadful noise behind me. It was the sound of a bicycle. I looked back. It was Pierre, a man old enough to be my father, if not my grandfather, cycling along seemingly without a care in the world, as if he were just popping out for a loaf of bread. Seeing me looking back he was out of the saddle, his tanned legs driving him closer and closer. If he passed me, could I follow? The despair, the feeling of stupidity at going too early, hit me. How could I have been so ignorant?

Then something glorious happened. There was a whirring and a crunching sound, the noise of gnarled gears. I quickly looked back to see Pierre off his bike, looking grim. I forced my speed up to 12 and sailed round the corner.

Whether Pierre's misfortune gave me wings I don't know, but I began to feel better. There was a bit of a plateau that allowed me to get up some pace. You pass a farm on your left, then you begin to climb again. Half an hour gone. Halfway surely.

No.

You may be more than halfway in distance, but not halfway in effort. There are neither trees nor vegetation up here to shield you from the sun. My water bottles were nearly empty now, but I knew I had to drink what little I had. A car passed me on a bend, sending a spray of diesel fumes into my face. There is a fine view back down into the valley, but you don't pause to stop on a bicycle, you just press on. There was no sign of my pursuers.

Eventually I passed a sign saying three kilometres. Just three more kilometres. That's nothing, I thought. That's the distance from the house to the village. It's a tiny distance that I don't even think about. I kept pedalling, desperately trying to maintain momentum and rhythm. Another sign. Two kilometres. My lungs were bursting now and my legs felt like I was underwater in a diving suit, weighed down with lead weights to stop me floating to the surface. The water bottles were empty now and the only moisture was the sweat that was pouring off my head. Some drops were getting in my eyes and stinging.

This bend must be the last, I thought. But it wasn't. There was always another. One kilometre to go. I passed a young couple walking down the hill. They waved and smiled, so I tried to look jolly, as if I were doing something that amused me. The desire now to stop the bike was intense. But I knew that if I ever stopped, I would never get back on again. Imagine the shame, to be overtaken pushing your bike up a hill? Besides, cycle shoes with their cleats are difficult to walk in.

Finally, the last corner. I could see a crossroads ahead of me, and a sign. One more turn of the pedals. Just one more turn. I allow myself a little look back. There is somebody there! Can I hold on? If I keep going they will not catch me. I try to rise from the saddle to give myself a bit of extra pace, but my body seems unwilling to do it. It knows I will get there as I am and seems happy with this. So I stay seated and reach the top. There is a memorial to members of the French Resistance, which throws a little shade. I prop the bike up and stretch out.

A rider appears. It is Lilliane, still looking fresh and relaxed.

'You're the first,' she says.

'Yes, but it nearly killed me.'

Charlie turns up soon behind her, then Pierre with a tale of missed gears and a slipping chain. He does not mention how he was catching me. Nor do I.

Up here the country is reminiscent of Scotland. There is heather, rounded hills and conifers. This used to be farming land, grazing for cattle and sheep. But the farmers gradually left the land, while the deforestation caused tremendous problems with flooding in the valley below. So the authorities turned the whole area into a national park, and planted trees.

When everybody had reached the top, we set off again. It was a short descent to Cambon, where we filled up our water bottles and laughed about the climb. Then we were off, past a trout stream, along a wooded road and past dry-stone walls. This took place at a good clip, and we were all anxious to show that we could keep up. Pierre in particular was forcing the pace, as if to show that if it were not for his chain, he would have been miles ahead by now.

We are gradually losing the other riders. Shouldn't we wait? Pierre explains that he climbs so fast because he doesn't like descending. You will see, he says. I wait in a lay-by at the top of the descent and let him go ahead of me. There is a wild hill of heather opposite. I expect to see deer and stalkers. Gerard shows up to tell me that you can sometimes see mountain sheep here. Then Claude whooshes past and we all follow.

I can get past Lilliane and Christian, but there is no way I can go as fast as Claude. Even though I try not to brake through the corners, keep the right line and tuck my body to make it as small as possible in the straights, he still keeps getting away from me. How is this possible? He must be braver than me, I think. So I try to leave my braking late, but I misjudge the scale of one corner, and am forced to lean over sharply to avoid going into the wall. Shit, that was close. How easy is it to fall off these bikes, I wonder? Unlike a motorbike, it doesn't seem like there is much contact between rubber and road.

If the climb is bad, the descent is almost worse. After a

while your neck begins to hurt, your shoulders ache, and your nerves are frayed. It goes on and on like a Russian novel until you want to sit up, stretch out, and stop. It's much longer than the climb we had just made, nearly 20 kilometres, although at speeds of 60 kilometres or more, it doesn't take too long.

Finally we all reach Lamalou-les-Bains. There is a small watering hole where we stop. The water is slightly fizzy, rather like Badoit. It is delicious. We haven't got far to go now. There is less than an hour's cycling, and it is familiar territory. We tuck in. I go behind Lilliane. She has the nicest legs. There is a nasty climb back up to Faugères, the same one that we came charging down four hours earlier. Pierre is leading and he suddenly ups the pace, so that we fall behind. I think I should go after him, but I don't really care any more whether he makes it up the hill before me or not.

Then it's downhill nearly all the way, back along the road where I walk the dogs, past the vineyards and the olive trees, and into the pool. I discover that I am very thirsty and hungry. Helena comes out to ask me if we had a good ride. Olivia shows up and says:

'You are mad.'

'Why?'

'Mummy says you are mad to go cycling.'

Floating in the pool, it is hard not to concede that she has a point.

Banyuls-sur-Mer, June 2003

Lipstick on a nun – the work of Odilon Redon –
marriage like a deep sea – running off with Van Goghs
– bottoms in the Tuileries gardens – Maillol becomes a
sculptor – winters in Banyuls-sur-Mer – the strong
body of a Russian girl – hiding refugees – painters in
Céret – who was Jean Moulin? – his cartoons in Béziers

I AM SITTING ON THE wall of one of the most beautiful cloisters in the world. The Abbaye de Fontfroide is a Cistercian monastery just west of Narbonne. It is as good an example of Romanesque architecture as you will find in the Languedoc. The cloister is square, with a stone floor and marble columns, some of which have been recently restored. Two of them were found in a house in Paris, and returned. Each arch rests on five sets of columns, their tops intricately carved with vines and heraldic designs, even water reeds, which were a symbol of the Cistercian Order, originally inspired by the lagoons in Burgundy.

The marble comes in many colours, some white, some pink, some red, rather like different varieties of wine. On top of the columns, before the barrel-vaulted ceiling, is a single round window like a porthole. The result is a feeling of lightness and air, as if the building were held up by belief and God's will alone. Here the monks would walk in silence, deep in contemplation. In the middle of the cloister there is a garden. An apricot-coloured rose climbs up the well in the centre. There are bright red geraniums in the border, rather incongruous, like a splash of red lipstick on the mouth of a nun.

Six hundred years ago this cloister would have been full of Cistercian monks, moving quietly from prayers to the library, or for meetings to discuss the running of the monastery. It was founded in 1093, as a Benedictine monastery. Fontfroide means literally 'cold spring', an ideal place to forge metal because the colder the water, the stronger the metal. It is tucked in the hills, sheltered from the winds, but just a short walk from the Via Domitia and the route to Spain. When Saint Bernard came to the Languedoc in 1145, he turned it into a Cistercian monastery. The Cistercians were a breakaway group of Benedictine monks, who felt that the teaching of Benedictine was not being closely observed. They emphasised agricultural work, scholarship and silence. They allowed lay brothers to live in parts of the monastery. They were required to do most of the heavy physical work, in return for eventual reward in heaven. In time the Cistercians became extraordinarily rich, with enormous holdings of land producing corn and wine and olives. When the Cathars were defeated, the monks became even more powerful, snatching land and property, their empire stretching to Catalonia, and including 25 enormous grain stores dotted around the countryside. With the possible exception of the Roman Empire, the Cistercians were the first of the great multinationals, with offices stretching throughout Europe. A giant cross on the hill above the monastery reminds you of who is in charge – like a Coca-Cola sign in Atlanta, or a statue of Stalin in Georgia.

The cloisters are now empty, except for a crowd of studious French academics who are examining every column in minute detail. Pushing past them, I found myself in a large church, with thick columns and a barrel-vault ceiling 20 metres high. We have left Romanesque and entered the Gothic Age. The clue is the height of the ceiling, and the shape of the roof. Somewhere, sometime in the 12th century, a monk or an architect managed to create an arch with a pointed top. At a stroke, covered spaces could be higher, more impressive, even awesome. The beauty of this church is its simplicity of design, built before Gothic art atrophied and turned into grotesque decoration, gargoyles and flying buttresses. Even so, as you pick out the details through the darkness, you notice something incongruous. In contrast to the austere architecture of the church, there are flamboyant stained glass windows. The Cistercians were renowned, at least in their early days, for restraint. They did not use stained glass, but grey glass. Outside the church, there is a statue and a painted figure of a lady. This also does not look quite right. Around a corner of the cloister there is a series of rooms, containing tapestries, large paintings by Richard Burgstahl and a kitchen full of copper pots. It is only when you climb upstairs to the library, and if you are lucky, go inside, that you realise what is going on here. Somewhere, between the French Revolution and now, the monastery fell into artistic hands. The library is a large room, complete with leather-bound books and a grand piano in one corner. But the clue is on the walls. There are two large murals, Night and Day. They were painted by Odilon Redon, the symbolist painter, who lived from 1840 to 1916.

Redon's murals in the library were left in place, along with the books. Many people consider them his finest work. He was born in Bordeaux, where as a young boy he would watch the clouds and imagine them to be figures from mythology. When he was 30 he moved to Paris, where, inspired by the work of Edgar Allan Poe and Baudelaire, he drew in charcoal strange figures such as insects and weird plants with human heads. He remained a relatively unknown figure until the publication of JK Huysmans' *A Rebours*, the tale of a decadent aristocrat. The hero, des Esseintes, collects the work of Redon. The French public was intrigued. They began to buy Redon's work as well.

He was just one of many artists, including Maillol and Matisse, who were lured to Fontfroide by Gustave Fayet, one of the Languedoc's most intriguing figures. The Fayet family made its money when it won the monopoly for shipping wine and brandy along the Canal du Midi. But Gustave's talents were not limited to making business deals. His interests were primarily artistic, although he was a shrewd investor of new talent, the Charles Saatchi of his day. He helped organise one of the first exhibitions of Picasso's art, which was held in Béziers in 1901. A friend and patron to young artists, he acquired more than 300 Impressionist paintings, including 20 Renoirs and 10 Gauguins, at a time when most people were denouncing the artists for their lack of ability.

Having been brought into the limelight, Redon's work changed. He started using pastels and oil, painting flowers and boats, buddhas and figures from mythology. Whether the colours and the flowers and the sunshine around Abbaye de Fontfroide played a part in his conversion to light from dark is not clear. He spent a lot of time walking in the hills, talking to other artists who stayed there. Both factors may have influenced him. It is intriguing that he decided to depict Night and Day in the library. Night shows a number of figures, including Madame Fayet, better known by her impressive maiden name of Madeleine d'Andoque de Sériège, and one of her daughters. They are painted turning away from each other, to reflect their lack of communication in real life. There are flowers, strange floating heads and fairies. Painted as if in a tile is a portrait of a lady. She is pretty, with her hair piled on her head. She was a nanny, whom

Gustave Fayet was particularly keen on. She wasn't allowed in the main part of the painting in case Madame Fayet was offended. The colours are sombre: blacks, blues and greys. On the other side of the room, Day shines with golden colours. The painting is dominated by four rearing horses against a backdrop of the Cévennes mountains. Again there are flowers, trees and butterflies, but they are red and yellow and green. The Chariot of Apollo was one of Redon's favourite themes. The chariot may not be here, but his horses are.

Fayet bought Abbaye de Fontfroide in 1908. It had been abandoned when the Cistercian monks fled for their lives in 1791, after the French Revolution. Eventually a small community of monks from Sénaque took over the place. When their leader, the abbot Père Jean, died in 1895, the abbey fell into disarray. The Bishop of Narbonne instructed neighbouring churches to help themselves to anything they wanted. Then Nelson Rockefeller's agents turned up to take the place stone by stone to his museum in New York. Could Gustave buy it and save it for France, asked the mayor of Béziers?

He could and he did. He filled it with his 300 Impressionist paintings. He invited his friends, including painters Odilon Redon and Daniel de Monfreid, together with composer Maurice Ravel to come and work and play in his abbey. Richard Burgstahl was hired to put stained glass in the empty windows that had been blown in by the wind.

Fayet lived there happily with his wife, until one day he caught her riding with his friend Monsieur Fabre. He had been telling Fabre that he should marry. 'Marriage is like jumping into a deep sea,' he told him. 'You just have to dive in and swim.' It turned out that his best friend decided that he would try out this marriage idea, but with Fayet's wife first. Gustave was mortified. He never spoke to Fabre or his wife again. He took his 300 Impressionist paintings – at one time he owned half of all the Van Goghs in the world – and moved north to a château near Paris, where he lived until his death shortly afterwards.

Next time you are in Paris, turn your back on the Louvre and IM Pei's pyramid, pass under the mini Arc de Triomphe that commemorates Napoleon's Italian cam-paign, and walk towards the Tuileries gardens. Almost immediately you will come to an area of box hedges, in which stands a collection of bronzed girls. They are quite short, with full thighs, big breasts and buttocks that are going slightly green, possibly from being stroked smooth by the hands of admiring passers-by. They are voluptuous, rounded, the bodies of peasant girls or lusty Greek goddesses.

Pomona stands with one apple in her left hand, and two smaller ones in her right. La Baigneuse se coiffant raises her right leg on a step, pushes out her breasts while her hands adjust her hair behind her head. Flora holds a garland of flowers draped over her thighs. Spring is the fairest and slimmest of all, with a small necklace of flowers, held over her breasts and beneath her chin.

They look best from the side view, their heads and shoulders raised above the hedge, behind them the horse chestnut trees and to the west, in the distance, the Eiffel Tower poking its head above the buildings. They are the work of Aristide Maillol.

If you cross the Seine and head into the 7th, you can visit a museum dedicated to his work and life. Here are his great sculptures of the first 40 years of the 20th century, as well as tapestries, gouaches, drawings and paintings, all dedicated to the same subject: plump, naked women. There are just a couple of works that depict characters with their clothes on. One is a painting of his aunt Lucie. She sits prim and erect on a wicker chair, dressed almost as a nun, in a long black dress and a bonnet, her long hands on her lap. Painted in 1892, it is the landscape that is most memorable: a couple of buildings, three tall trees rather like cypresses, with the mountains behind. It is not French, nor even Italian. It is Catalan.

He was born Aristide Bonaventure Jean Maillol on December 8, 1861 in Banyuls-sur-Mer, the last seaside resort in France before you reach Spain. He was the fourth of five children. His father, Raphaël, was a shopkeeper, who did a lot of business with Algeria, and travelled frequently to the country. He grew up not with his parents and siblings, but with his aunt Lucie. It is not clear why this happened. Perhaps it was financial; or perhaps she was lonely. Either way, Aristide had a rather solitary childhood, spending much of his early years with his blind grandfather, whom he would lead around the town so that he could meet his old friends. They spent their time talking about smuggling and fishing, with little Aristide sitting on his knee and listening.

At 13, he was sent away to boarding school in Perpignan. He found it boring. A sign of homesickness is that when he paints his first picture, it is a view of the port of Banyuls. The death of his father three years later hits the family income. Worse is to follow. Phylloxera destroys the family vineyard, and with it their last remaining source of income. He is expelled from school and returns to Banyuls. Determined to be an artist, he spends his time producing a magazine called *La Figue*, which is later renamed *Le Journal d'un Ennuyé*, or the diary of a bored person. He is the magazine's only writer, illustrator, editor, printer and reader. He produced 20 copies, none of which survives.

In 1881, bolstered by a small allowance from his aunt Lucie, he leaves for Paris to study art. He rents a room in the rue des Vertus and eats meals with his former primary school teacher at 10 rue des Gravilliers. He makes several attempts to pass the entrance exams for the Ecole des Beaux Arts, but is unsuccessful. Instead, he enrols in the antique drawing classes run by Gérome, a painter and sculptor. Maillol shows him his work. 'You know nothing!' he is told. 'Go and enrol in the Ecole des Arts Décoratifs and work on noses and ears.'

To begin with he ignores this advice, and continues hanging around the classes, where one of his few friends is Achille Laugé, a fellow southerner who is also trying to make it as a painter in Paris. Finally he takes Gérome's advice and goes to the Ecole des Arts Décoratifs, where he proves to be a good student. Four years later, on March 17, 1885, he passes the examination for the Ecole des Beaux Arts. He spends five years there, frequenting museums and copying the work of the great masters. But he is disappointed with the teaching. When asked what he learnt there, he replies: 'Nothing.' Perhaps paralysed with conflicting advice, it takes him three years to produce one painting.

At the end of the 1880s he is surviving on a meagre grant from the Conseil Général of his department. He visits an exhibition by the Impressionists at the Café Volpini, which includes the work of Van Gogh, Emile Bernard and Paul Gauguin. 'Gauguin's painting was a revelation,' he said later. 'Instead of enlightening me, the Ecole des Beaux Arts had thrown a veil over my eyes. Standing in front of the Pont-Aven paintings, I had a feeling that I too could work in that spirit. Right then I told myself that what I did would be good when it had Gauguin's approval.'

By 1892 he becomes interested in tapestry making, spending hours at the Cluny Museum. Back in Banyuls, he sets up a tapestry workshop, employing two sisters, Angélique and her older sister Clotilde Narcisse. They make their own colours from plants and rocks that he gathers from walks on the mountainsides. He returns to Paris, accompanied by Clotilde, and they set up home together. He paints her portrait in 1894. She has dark hair, red eyes and the expression of a cat. For the moment, she keeps her clothes on. He is still obsessed by his tapestries, but the work puts a severe strain on his eyes, and makes him go temporarily blind. He decides to give up tapestry. He is now nearly 40. For 20 years he has worked as a painter, achieving only limited success. Suddenly he turns to sculpting.

On a shelf on the second floor of the Maillol museum sits a small wood carving, no more than 12 inches high. It is called La Source, and shows the figure of a naked woman, possibly Clotilde. It looks like she is clutching a dress or a sheet to her waist and it is billowing out behind her, but more probably, it is water. Already, it is classic Maillol. There is nothing pretty here, in contrast to his paintings. She is a robust woman, with well-rounded buttocks and firm thighs. His brother, Adolphe Simon, had been a wood carver. He died when Maillol was just 10. But did the young Aristide learn the technique from him?

From wood he moved to bronze, starting with small figures. In 1900 he produces nearly 30 statuettes. There is a portrait of him painted around this time by Jozsef

Rippl-Ronai, which now hangs in the Musée d'Orsay. He is wearing a straw hat and the sort of long, black beard that you might use to disguise yourself if you were a cartoon character and planning to rob a bank. The most striking features are the rather long, thin pointed nose and the bright eyes. They give him a vulpine air.

His first one man show in 1902 wins him praise from the art critic Octave Mirbeau, who buys one of his bronzes, and writes that everybody else should do the same. By 1905 when he exhibits *La Méditerranée*, his career takes off. André Gide praises him for breathing new life into sculpture; Maurice Denis draws a line from the Greeks through Gothic Art to Maillol. Count Kessler, a German who is one of Europe's richest men, becomes his patron.

What is it about *La Méditerranée* that got everybody so excited? Clotilde was the model for a series of versions. The first, made in 1902, shows a woman with coiffed hair sitting on the ground. Her right arm is back to take her weight. Her left arm is resting on her left knee. She is heavy, rooted, but not ponderous. She exudes calm. A second version, made between 1902 and 1905, sits in the trees in the Tuileries gardens. The left arm is folded now, resting on her left knee and her head, as if sitting for so long has made her reflective, or just tired. It is as if she has been sitting there forever. His women are not Clotilde, or Dina or anybody else. They are more abstract than that. Maillol himself said that he was not the man for a formal portrait. He was creating something timeless. Instead of a specific woman, he was creating woman.

This is one of the reasons the critics raved. Maillol had freed sculpture from the clutter of much 19th century French work by creating something more refined. In the process he stilled the clamour of France's most popular sculptor of the time, Auguste Rodin. French writer André Gide called Maillol the inventor of silence in sculpture. Another French writer, Claude Roy, said, rather verbosely: 'Rodin invented a speechless universe filled with a thousand shouts, and the wordless mouths of the creatures he gave birth to will never stop grasping their unappeasable wail of woe throughout time. Maillol opens the gates of an orchard's realm of silence, where shrilling cicadas and murmuring springs weave their torpid terror round Eve and invisible Adam.'

Having found this 'orchard' Maillol continued to pursue it for the rest of his career, concentrating mainly on female nudes. But he never escaped the influence of the Roussillon coast and its mountains. Even once he started becoming famous and receiving commissions, Maillol divided his time between a house in Marly-le-Roi on the outskirts of Paris, where he spent the summers, and Banyuls-sur-Mer, where he wintered. Maillol went on a visit to Greece in his 40s. He said that the landscape was very familiar. It reminded him of where he grew up. In Banyuls he bought a farmhouse called La Métairie. There is a river at the bottom of the garden, choked with tiny white and yellow flowers. The air is heavy with their scent. Poppies and wild flowers grow on the banks. It is a place that Ophelia might have chosen to drown. Surrounding the property is a series of hills. They rise until they become a mountain, rugged and stern, blocking the skyline, topped only by a brooding cloud. Each patch of hill is marked by an assortment of activity: here there are terraced vineyards, divided by drystone walls. Occasionally there will be a diagonal water course, designed to rush the heavy rainfall away from the plants. Below the vines sits an olive grove, leaves tousled in the wind. Further up the hill the vegetation disappears, until there is nothing but rocks and pine trees. At the top of one of the hills looking east is a small white church. It is Greece.

Maillol adored the landscape. Art and the countryside of his birth were his two passions in life. 'Some days I spend hours without moving on a chaise longue,' he told his friend François Bassères. 'I could stay for days in the countryside. Here everything is so calm, so soothing. Next to me is some paper. From time to time I'll take the crayon and I'll draw an idea. Then back to rest.' His friends say that his success did not change him. The only thing that improved was the quality of wine and food at his table.

In the 1930s his career received a late fillip. He heard of a girl who would make the perfect model. He wrote her a letter: 'Mademoiselle, I am told you look like a Maillol or a Renoir. I would settle for a Renoir.' There is a rather poignant aside in AJ Liebling's *Between Meals* on this topic. Liebling's eating friend Yves Mirande falls ill over lunch and he has to take him home. Mirande shows him his art collection: 'All the sculptures are by Renoir,' he said. 'It was his hobby. And all the paintings are by Maillol. It was his hobby. If it were the other way around, I would be one of the richest chaps in France. Both men were my friends. But then, one doesn't give one's friends one's bread and butter. And, after all, it's less banal as it is.'

The model, Dina Vierny, turned out to be more Maillol than Renoir. There is a photo of her taken when she was 17. She is naked, covered only in her long, curly hair. You can understand why a sculptor would be tempted to write to her. She was well built, powerful, with large breasts, a curvy body and a smile. In some of the paintings that he did of her, such as *Le Grand Nu Jaune* and *Les Deux Dina*, I was reminded of the paintings of the Soviet era, showing strong peasant women working in the fields. In fact, Dina was of Russian ancestry.

The last statue he was working on is called *Harmony*. A figure of a young girl, with relatively slim hips and pert breasts. He works on the statue for more than four years, modelling and remodelling, destroying versions that fail to please him. Dina Vierny joins him in Banyuls, where at last he is happy with four plaster versions: a headless standing torso; a torso with a head; a head with detail of the hair; and a mask. 'I want this work to be more realist and alive than anything I have done up until now,' he says.

He is also busy on other projects. Vierny is helping him to catalogue his work. On dark nights she is also leading refugees to safety in Spain, via a path that Maillol is said to have shown her, thus avoiding the French border controls. It is nice to think of the ageing artist in his beret leading his buxom model up a steep and windy path to help the heroes of the resistance. He lends Vierny his studio in the village of Puig del Las to hide people. The network is known as the 'Réseau Maillol'.

On September 15, 1944, he sets out in a car to visit his friend Raoul Dufy. It is raining. On a sharp windy bend, the car skids and overturns. Maillol is badly injured and after a lengthy delay, is taken home. He lives on for another 12 days, then dies. *Harmony* will never have hands.

Achille Laugé, his friend from his Paris days, died that same year. His career was not as exalted as Maillol's, but he continued working, painting pictures of flowers, the boats at Collioure, the road through the Genets. Maillol is buried in the shade of some cypress trees, under his bronze *La Méditerranée*, in the garden of his house in Banyuls.

One of Maillol's closest friends was Henri Matisse. Matisse would come and help Maillol in the studio, applying water to his plaster casts and, on at least one occasion, applying so much that the arm fell off. The friendship survived. Matisse, partly inspired by his friend, decided to spend some time in Collioure in the summer of 1905. He settled in to the Hôtel de la Gare and invited André Derain, a fellow painter, to join him. Matisse was bored with pointillisme – as anyone who looks at more than one painting in that style often becomes. On holiday the two friends grew fascinated by the colours, the light, the shadows and the water. Collioure then was just a poor fishing village.

Matisse and Derain returned to Paris with nearly 50 paintings and exhibited them together with work by Albert Marquet and Charles Camoin. The critics were harsh. 'Savagery', 'wild animals', 'clashing colours', they shrieked. The painters were dubbed the 'Fauves' or wild beasts, after the critic Louis Vauxcelles remarked of a painting: 'It's like Donatello in a cage of wild beasts.' The sun had gone to their head and affected their palettes. Their works that summer and the following year are marked by a bold use of colour, partly inspired by Gauguin and Van Gogh. Raoul Dufy also paints there after the Second World War. In one of his notebooks is a sketch of the barques catalanes of Collioure and the comment underneath: 'Collioure sans voiles, c'est une nuit sans étoiles.' Sadly the fishing boats are no longer there, banned by a bossy mayor who did not want them to interfere with the bathing habits of tourists.

Artists also gathered slightly inland from Collioure at Céret. Céret is a pretty town with narrow streets, shaded by giant plane trees, famous for its cherry trees that ripen in early April. A Spanish artist, Manolo Hugué, was the first to live there. He invited his friends to visit, Juan Gris, Max Jacob and Pablo Picasso. Here Picasso and Georges Braque refined cubism together. There is a fine museum of modern art in the middle of the town. Designed with verve by the Catalan architect Jaime Freixa, the gallery is a series of good-sized rooms and coloured walls. One of the highlights of the permanent collection is the series of ceramic bowls created by Picasso in a frenzied week in April in 1953. Each bowl becomes the arena. On the edges the crowd and the flags. In the middle the sun shines, and the bull and the matadors fight to the death. Upstairs there is a stylish terrace, with terracotta armchairs, a sofa and tables, sunblind to match, overlooking the rooftops of Céret.

In the fine art museum in Béziers, the atmosphere is rather different. There is a rather mixed collection of art from the 18th and 19th centuries. But you are no longer in a modern Catalan museum but back in 19th century France. The building is grand and ghastly. If you ask nicely, you might be allowed to see the collection of drawings by Béziers' most famous son, Jean Moulin. He is not honoured for his painting skills in other museums or collections, but he is famous throughout France, as a hero of the Resistance. Just about every French town has a school, a square or an avenue named after him. Typically Béziers does not make a big deal of this. The only memorial to him is a rather ghastly modern sculpture hidden away in the Jardin des Poètes. A figure, presumably intended to be Moulin, sits naked with a straight back, looking as if he is trying to break some firewood over his knee. On closer inspection it turns out to be a sword. The character has curly hair and a muscled upper body. The inscription reads: *A Jean Moulin, fils de Béziers, organisateur de la Résistance, Héros et martyr. A ses frères en sacrifice.*

But who was Jean Moulin? For 20 years after the Second World War, he was a forgotten man. His birth as a public figure dates from a cold December day in 1964. André Malraux, author of *La Condition Humaine* and a politician in General de Gaulle's government, gave a speech. It was a moment of high passion. Isaiah Berlin called the performance 'an unforgettable evocation of what the Resistance had been'. In front of Malraux stood the coffin of Moulin, draped in grey cloth, the edges blowing up in the chill wind. Opposite, the tall, beak-nosed Charles de Gaulle, in military uniform. Around him, other survivors of the Resistance movement. Sombre music played. Above it, the shrill voice of Malraux.

'Twenty years have passed since Jean Moulin became the leader of a people of the night. Without this ceremony how many of the children of France would even recognise his name?' By now many of the audience were in tears, only de Gaulle remaining impassive. It did not matter that the coffin was almost empty, that Moulin's body had never been found, that nobody really knew the truth of what happened to him when he disappeared in 1943. 'Think of his poor, battered face, of those lips that never spoke. That day, his last day, it was the face of France.'

Jean Moulin was born on June 20 1899, the son of a schoolteacher, who taught French history and literature in the same classroom for 50 years. They lived in an apartment overlooking the Champs de Mars in Béziers. He passed an uneventful childhood. The most exciting thing was probably watching the wine demonstrations in 1907 out of the window. He went to his father's school, where he quickly became a rebel, struggling through his exams, until he was called up for military service in 1918. Although he was sent to the front after training in Montpellier, he did not see a shot fired. The armistice came. He was demobbed, and went to study law in Montpellier. He became a civil servant. Suddenly ambitious, he is made sub-mayor of Albertville in the Savoie. This marks the end of his link with the Languedoc, although he continues to visit his parents. As well as skiing, he makes sketches and cartoons, publishing his work under the pseudonym Romanin. The name comes from the château near the family's ancestral house in the village of Saint-Andiol in Provence.

When Moulin came to play a role in the Resistance, he opened an art gallery in Nice, operating it under the name of Romanin. For Ffr100,000 he bought two paintings by Degas, one by Suzanne Valadon, and one by Maillol's friend Raoul Dufy. Then he travelled to London, where eventually he fell under the spell of General de Gaulle. He was sent back to France with the mission of reconciling the different factions of the Resistance, and hoping to persuade them to fight the Nazis instead of each other.

On the longest day of 1943, Jean Moulin was sitting in a doctor's office in Caluire, a suburb of Lyon, waiting to meet fellow members of the Resistance. Instead, Klaus Barbie and his Gestapo burst through the door, and arrested all seven men. Moulin was interrogated. Members of the Resistance have claimed that they saw him three more times alive, once in Lyon and twice in the villa occupied by SS Major Karl Boemelburg, the head of the Gestapo in France. His face was said to be covered in blood. His death certificate states that he died in Metz, still in France but close to the German border, probably of head injuries. There is no sign that he talked or betrayed his colleagues. But there is no evidence to the contrary. He was the perfect symbol of the Resistance, who could occupy the same role as the Unknown Soldier. In the meantime, he could be a hero. France's shame could be buried along with his coffin.

Moulin's birthplace Béziers is the kind of town that most people bypass on holiday. It is wild and chaotic, rather like its one-way system, which sucks you in and spits you out somewhere miles from where you want to be if you make just one wrong turn. The town has a Spanish feel, shown in its love of bullfighting and its ramblas, a smaller version of Barcelona's magnificent pedestrian street. Here in the shade of giant plane trees, you can saunter among the flower stalls, take lunch at the small bars and restaurants if you have three hours to kill, and admire the city's beautiful women.

Back in the Art Museum there is a new exhibition dedicated to Moulin. His sister Laure donated more than 500 of his art works and numerous notebooks to the place. The early work shows watercolours of Béziers, sketches of schoolfriends and caricatures of teachers. In May 1921 his was the winning design for a poster to celebrate the 10th meeting of the national union of students in the city. It shows a red-hatted troubadour on a black horse blowing a trumpet. Once he began to move with a fashionable set, he drew the places he went, such as night clubs in Paris and society weddings and funerals. In a covered table in the Béziers museum is a sketch called *A beautiful funeral: waiting for the funeral*. The widow, an attractive woman in her late 20s or early 30s, is applying make-up and looking at herself in the mirror, more interested in her appearance than the burial of her dead husband. Waiting outside, the funeral cortège, severe in their top hats. I think you would appreciate the irony.

Sainte Cécile, September 2003

The colour green – when the wind drops – the pizza
vans – the best strawberries you will ever eat – making
waves – lights go out on Christmas Eve – nettles in
hedgerows – eating a peach – a visit to the hills – more
boars than bores – the mighty Orb – a winemaker's
wife from Macclesfield – we don't get to Lodève – a
romantic evening in Château Coujan, accompanied
by peacocks and guitars

IT IS THREE YEARS since I first started writing to you about this place and its people. Now that you are moving down here, there will be no need to keep you informed on such a regular basis. Soon I can take you around and show you all the sites I have described, and see them anew through your eyes. But have I told you all you need to know? Have I missed something, or misled you? Do you have a sense of the place? Could you paint it?

The colours are interesting here. At first it seems a rather dull landscape, particularly when the sun is not shining. The houses do not have the immediate charm of those in Provence. There is less decoration. Less colour.

The traditional colour of the shutters is a green, a slightly darker version of the colour used by Penguin books in their series of Twentieth Century Classics. It works well with the houses, the trees, the light. At its best it looks like the underside of the leaves of the olive tree.

There is a book called *Les Couleurs de la France*, written by Jean Philippe Lenclos and his wife Dominique. It is now out of print, but it is a work of serious research, gained from a lifetime of study on the traditional materials used to decorate the houses of France. Lenclos and his team produced palettes of typical facades – doors, windows and walls – all painstakingly coloured to show the tones and shades of each region. He visited many of the river beds and quarries. When he had determined the exact colour shades that he deemed acceptable, he went to the local authorities and tried to persuade them to make his recommendations law. In some cases he was successful. Unfortunately he did not get as far as the Languedoc, but he did visit Provence and made some interesting observations on the dominant styles of the region.

Lenclos's view is that because of the harsh Mediterranean sun, which tones down many of the colours, and the multitude of different people who have lived and passed through the area, each county has its own customs and traditions. The main colours are beige, yellows, reds or pinks, derived from chalk or render or whitewash. These colours have also moved along the coast, although in the

Languedoc there is also a Catalan influence of orange. But it is the Languedoc green that predominates.

Not long after reading this book I was flicking through a newspaper when I discovered a report presented to the American Astronomical Society. Apparently two scientists, Dr Karl Glazebrook of John Hopkins University and his colleague Dr Ivan Baldry, analysed data from more than 200,000 galaxies between two and three billion light years from earth. The scientists combined information from visible light wavelengths, transforming it into an array of colours visible to the human eye. They discovered that if all the light in the universe were passed through a prism it would produce a colour somewhere between 'aquamarine and turquoise'. Dr Glazebrook told the assembled astronomers that he had been surprised by the result. 'From one perspective, it's surprising, because there are no green stars. But it's the large number of old red stars and young blue stars in the universe that gives us the green.' There was a small patch of colour next to the story, like a pantone that you use when you try to pick a colour to paint a wall. It matched exactly the colour of a Languedoc shutter. You wonder who pays for this kind of research and if they think they are getting value for money. (Some weeks later I read a correction to this story. The astronomers had recalculated and discovered that rather than Languedoc green, the universe was a sort of grey-beige colour. Rather more prosaic, even if accurate.)

Have I warned you about the wind? Strangely enough, you notice it most when it doesn't blow. Earlier today I was walking around the garden, checking the pool and the plants, admiring the roses, when I realised something was missing. But everything seemed to be in place; everything was in order. The olive trees are growing slowly, the cypresses are standing to attention like soldiers. Then it dawned on me: the bambouserie was not rustling. The trees were not moving. The wind had died.

Sometimes it can blow for days at a time and rattles the shutters. Here there are two main winds. The Tramontane comes from the north, bringing clear skies, drying the vines and the land like a hair dryer. The Marin comes from the sea. It brings a sea mist, clouds and rain. Fortunately, the prevailing wind is from the north.

In the autumn the swallows, preparing for their long flight to Africa, practise aerobatics, racing one moment with the wind then battling into it in the opposite direction. On calmer evenings at dusk the swallows can be seen drinking from the pool. This also is an acrobatic feat, accomplished only by the very skilful, for they must bank steeply, turn then make sure they do not drink too deeply from the pool or they will stall and crash. If you are lucky you can watch them – one evening I sat in the shade of a pine tree and observed their antics – but they scare easily, and are particularly nervous of the cat.

As well as providing a wind tunnel for migratory birds, the wind also dries the ground. However much it rains –

and winter storms can bring four or five centimetres a night – there is seldom any mud. The wind dries the ground in a day or so. The wind also blows the clouds away. It is the cool north wind that is the most benign, for it ensures sunny days, scaring away any clouds that dare to drift over the horizon. In contrast the wind from the south is warm, but it brings humidity, almost a sea fog, that is dank and unpleasant.

When the wind blows from the south it also brings the sound of the village. You may catch a snatch of music from the tannoy, followed by the disembodied voice from the Mairie: 'Allo! Allo! Le marchand de coquillage est sur la place!' Or on Thursday evenings: 'Mesdames et messieurs, Chez Jojo est sur la place.' Chez Jojo is the pizza van. Pizza vans are unique to the south of France. The van itself is crummy, peeling paint of red and cream, but the pizzas are superb, as if the driver had raced pell-mell from Naples that evening, with the margaritas still warm.

On Wednesdays the voice announces the arrival of the market. This is a market that is almost minimalist in its simplicity. There will probably be Bruno, selling whatever fruit or vegetables happen to be in season. There is the greengrocer, who has an enormous stock of every kind of fruit or vegetable you can imagine. His wife is a keen cook, and swaps recipes with Helena. For two weeks running there was an Italian cheese-man, who appeared with a Dutch girlfriend. Then they stopped coming and never reappeared. There is often a meat van, selling saucisson, pâtés and tripe. Depending on the season, a random van will show up. Sometimes it will be selling beds or mattresses; other times plastic Christmas trees. There is an old lady who sells bundles of asparagus freshly picked from her garden. Later in the year she sells garriguette strawberries that are the sweetest and best strawberries you will ever eat.

It is the sun not the wind that draws people to the south of France. It is said that Montpellier gets more than 300 days of sunshine a year. This is surely the work of an ambitious marketing person. In my experience, it is less than that. But there are summer days when the sun is a constant factor. It gets so you begin to look for shade, to park the car or even when you sit and take a coffee. This for a person from the north is a revelation. How you will find it compared to Yorkshire will be interesting to watch. How many days of sunshine do you get a year in Yorkshire? Three? Anyway, I have sometimes begun to wonder whether the clouds of the north aren't even a blessing in disguise. This heat can sap the mind, slow the body, make any movement a serious challenge. It is no surprise that northerners, huddled in their coats and cities, look down on the south as an indolent, sensual place, full of loose morals and flabby, sun-fried minds. The only thing that saves us is the lack of humidity.

Some friends bought a house nearby and spent nearly a year renovating it. They moved down in June, during a heatwave. The husband has fair English skin. He spent most of the days hiding in cafés. In the evenings he was so scared of being bitten by mosquitoes that he kept the windows and shutters tightly closed. It was hot in the house, unbearably hot. The wife would phone me in the mornings, complaining that maybe she had found the wrong house or the wrong husband. But then on that second sweltering night she happened to brush against one of the newly installed radiators. It was on. When the sun had stopped cooking the house the central heating had kicked in. They managed to turn it off, and so far, both the house and the marriage have remained intact.

The first September we were here produced the most splendid weather I have ever encountered. At eight o'clock in the morning it was still fresh, almost cool. We would drink tea on the terrace, but still wear a sweater. Minutes later the sun would appear over the hill, then begin its epic journey across the sky. It was untroubled by clouds. It was not until the evening that its power began to fade.

The winter storms came as a shock. The river bed at the foot of the valley suddenly turned into a stream, then a torrent. Each day as we went to get bread the water rose, until one morning it was beginning to lap over the bridge. All that day it rained, and all night too. In the morning the post did not arrive. We walked down to the bridge to find that the river was now a lake. The bridge had disappeared under two feet of water. Helena crossed it in her Wellington boots, cautiously because you had to be sure you were stepping on the bridge and not into the river. Then we walked back to the house for lunch, cut off from the world like a pair of medieval monarchs behind their moat.

The rain did not stop that night either, so in the morning I felt obliged to cross the bridge in the car. I persuaded Helena that the journey was a necessity.

'We need provisions,' I said. 'This rain could last for days.'

'We have plenty of food in the freezer.'

'I need fresh bread. Milk for the children.'

'There is milk in the freezer.'

There was no reason for the crossing, but it was a challenge. She thought it was madness to risk losing the car in the maelstrom. As an afterthought, she expressed some concern for my safety.

'If you were to walk in front of me, you can point out the way.'

'Bugger off.'

She decided not to come and watch the crossing of the ford. I sped down the drive, splashing through the puddles, then slowed up as I got nearer the river. I edged the car to the water. The current was strong, bringing branches and debris from upstream. What if I were caught like that tree and deposited upside down on the other bank? This was no way to think. I had read somewhere that the key in such a situation was to select a low gear and keep revving: that way no water could get into the engine. I set off, creating my own tidal wave, which threatened to break over the bonnet, but disappeared once we reached the other side. I felt strangely exultant, and at the same time, rather silly.

I felt sure that Béatrice in the bread shop would be impressed that I had managed to make it to the village, but she seemed preoccupied and unwilling to chat. I bought all sorts of provisions – cans of peas and carrots, cat food, dog food, bottles of wine – in order to make the journey seem worthwhile, and retraced my steps across the river.

This kind of adventure is an essential part of country living. It sets you apart from the city dwellers, whose only problems are taxi drivers who turn up late or take the wrong route. But water, light and heating are seldom interrupted in the cities. Hit a switch and light appears. Turn a tap and you have running water. However, the winter rain wreaked havoc with our electrics. In the run-up to Christmas the house seemed haunted by an evil genie. Every morning we would put on a couple of heaters, boil a kettle, turn on the radio and – bang! – the lights would go out. It took a couple of frustrating weeks of darkness and candles and wondering what on earth we were doing living in a foreign country in the middle of nowhere without light or water, when suddenly Helena had a bright idea.

'Maybe this electricity problem was caused by the electrician,' she said.

We had tried a number of electricians. The first was charming, vague, looked a bit like Dustin Hoffman. He went on holiday to Cuba in the middle of a rewiring job and never came back. The second electrician came with a priceless asset: a knowledge of English. We could tell him things and he would understand. It was his idea to fit a trip switch to the electricity supply. There was no question that it worked. Hit the wrong switch and we were immediately condemned to ten frustrating minutes of fumbling in the cellar, turning all the fuses off, waiting, then putting them back on, one by one. It was here that the evil genie had most fun. Some mornings it would be the heater in the kitchen that tripped the switch; other days it was the kettle, or the fridge.

I phoned the electrician. 'You need to come and get rid of this trip switch,' I said.

'Eeze dangerous,' he said.

'It will be more dangerous if you don't.'

We were planning a big Christmas Eve party. This is the night when Christmas is celebrated in Sweden. Presents are opened, the tree is dressed, and there is general goodwill to all men. Elaborate preparations had been made. The Christmas tree in the garden had been cut down and brought inside. Strange food – mainly Swedish, consisting of herring, caviar in a tube of toothpaste, large wheels of dry Ryvita-type bread, meatballs, porridge – had been ordered because my wife is half Swedish. Guests were invited for seven o'clock. At six o'clock, with the rain beating down, we started to get ready. Minutes later the lights went out. I went through the elaborate fuse box routine. Nothing. We called the electrician on a mobile phone, and lit candles. The candles threw giant shadows on the walls. An hour later the first guests arrived and congratulated us on the authentic Swedish atmosphere. Then the electrician arrived. For 20 minutes I followed him around with a torch while he fiddled with fuses. Each time he manipulated the trip switch, but each time it tripped. It was Bea's first Christmas. At this rate she would spend it in the dark.

'Why don't you just take the trip switch off,' said Helena.

'It's very dangerous,' I said. 'The electrician told me that without the trip switch, if I were to touch the washing machine I might die.'

'I don't know why that would bother you. You never touch the washing machine anyway. Gaspard: take the trip switch off.'

The electrician did as he was told. The electrics came back on. We wished him a Merry Christmas, gave him a glass of Aquavit, and sent him on his way. We made a New Year's resolution to find another electrician. Then we turned all the lights off and lit the candles again, because it looked better that way.

It is the quiet moments that count. The walks in the hills among the garrigue, each footstep scented by crushed thyme. Overhead a couple of buzzards soar. A hoopoe – a brown and white bird with a mohican hair cut that comes from Africa for a few months – flies off a telegraph wire and shows us his crown with pride. The dog covers the ground in huge swathes, tail like a rudder through the tall grass. Sometimes she puts up a partridge or a woodcock. Once, memorably, she surprised a hare, which took off over the hill at speed.

Some afternoons we run into an old couple. Depending on the season, they are looking for mushrooms, fruit, nuts or wild asparagus. There is no shortage of edible things to find on the walk: almonds, blackberries, apples, pears, apricots, peaches and chestnuts on the high ground. And of course everywhere there are grapes, some bitter and tainted by a spray, but many are sweet. When we lived in Sussex, the only things that were edible in the hedgerows were nettles.

It is not just that these foods are available. It is how good they taste. For example, a peach. A good peach in England is a difficult thing to find. Often they taste like cricket balls, hard and furry. But here, they are different. First, there is the fun of picking it. The trees are quite like apple trees, with rather frilly leaves. You take the peach and hold it in your hand. The skin is soft, with a mottled colour. At the top, where it hung from the tree, it is yellow. But elsewhere it is a blend of red and oranges, mixed like an impressionist painting. The smell is intoxicating. It is honey sweet. You bite into it. Some people peel the skins of peaches, but I like the mixture of soft flesh and firm skin. It is a taste of sunshine, a taste of summer. Juice dribbles down my chin. Do I dare to eat a peach? I do.

At one time most of the landscape must have been cultivated. There are huge outcrops of stone that have been piled on top of each other, cleared to make a field or vineyard. Wild herbs and trees now grow in these fields, but the boundaries remain visible. By one of these fields is a stunning drystone wall. In the evening sunlight it glows with a deep warmth. Whoever built this wall is long dead, or no longer working, as this technique is lost to the area, but his craft endures, a testimony to honest endeavour. Parts are falling down due to heavy rains or stone robbers, but most of it is beautiful enough to grace any museum in the world. Instead it stands unnoticed by a small vineyard, waiting until it falls down or is taken down.

It is not just the countryside that is deserted in the winter. At times the towns and villages appear empty, as if the inhabitants have emigrated abroad along with the swallows. The people have not disappeared, but they may be hiding. There is a local saying: Pour vivre heureux, vivons cachés. To live well, you have to be hidden. There is very little ostentatious show of wealth. The cars are as poor as those on the streets of eastern Europe or Wales. Occasionally you will see a sports car, a Porsche or Ferrari, but these will be visiting wine buyers, en route to somewhere else. Most of the French live in fear of the taxman. Apparently France has a higher percentage of people turning in their neighbours for suspected tax abuse than anywhere else in Europe. This is why the clever ones are careful never to let on the amount of money that they have hidden under their mattresses.

One notable absence for a visitor from the north is the lack of animals in the fields. It is partly the heat that cleared the fields, but also the railways. The iron horse spelt the end of marginal vineyards in areas such as Orléans and its surrounding countryside. They simply could not compete with the yield that was possible in the south. In return for the barrels of wine they were receiving, the northerners sent down cheeses and meat, making the tough task of rearing animals in an arid climate nonsensical. At one time there was the trans-humance, the movement of animals every spring and autumn from the Pyrénées and the High Languedoc to the plain. Each animal would wear a collar with a bell fashioned from bone around its neck. It is nice to imagine them walking along, ringing their bells like a choir at Christmas.

In the Camargue, Jacques Bon has an enormous thatched barn that used to house up to 5,000 sheep. The interior is splendid, with low walls and a magnificent vaulted wooden ceiling. The animals were moved on foot from the Camargue to the hills, a walk of over 100 kilometres spread over a number of days. Then they were loaded onto trains and taken to new pastures. When this became uneconomic, they were put onto buses. Now the sheep are gone altogether, sold when Britain was allowed to join the common market. Instead the interior is filled with business men and wedding parties. One Frenchman I spoke to recalled the days when a trainload of sheep were marched up Béziers High Street, through the allées and running into the fountains. This was during the war, to avoid the train station and the attention of the hungry Gestapo.

One day we ventured up into the hills to see what it was like. This is not a place one normally goes. Everything seems to happen down on the coast or the plain, but not far away is another country. I thought it would be interesting to see what happens up there. And whenever the coastal roads are full of Dutch cars pulling caravans you know it is time to take to the hills.

As soon as you pass the petrol station that sells wine at the top of Faugères, the landscape changes completely. There are rolling hills, chestnut trees and the sound of running water. There are fewer houses, just a few hilltop villages made of stone with pitched roofs. It is said that there are more wild boars up here than people.

This is a place people have gone for generations to hide. First the Cathars hid from the Catholics in these hills; then the Protestants came here after the Edict of Nantes was revoked and religious freedom in France was no longer tolerated. It is hard to know what people are hiding from nowadays. Maybe their first wives or the taxman, or both.

The Haut Languedoc is like a ridge that looks over the plain towards the sea. It is from here that the three great rivers that bring so much life to the region begin, the Hérault, the Orb and the Aude. Although the Orb is probably the least celebrated – at any rate it does not have a département named after it – it is my favourite. It is a great river for canoeing; it runs beside the golf course in Lamalou-Les-Bains, so no doubt it washes a great quantity of my golf balls to the sea; and it flows serenely through Béziers, watching without demur the wild events of that city.

We followed the road by the river Orb north to Lodève. The landscape changes quickly, dramatically. There is a pause in the climb at Hérépian, an unremarkable town except for its Musée de la Cloche et de la Sonnaille. Here at the foundry, bells have been made for 400 years.

Before you reach Lodève you pass through Tour sur Orb. It is a small inconsequential place, the sort of place you notice only as you leave it and you wonder briefly what it would be like to live there but you don't have time to stop. But in the marketplace on that Thursday were stalls and umbrellas and people tasting food and drink. We decided to park up and discover what was going on. We had probably turned up on the most auspicious day in Tour sur Orb's undistinguished history. It turned out that all the winemakers had sent supplies of Cartagène, a rather curious local liquor made of alcohol and grape juice, to Paris for the first time to be judged by the Ministry of Agriculture and Fishery. A gold medal had been won by a local winemaker in Tour sur Orb and that is why the party was being held in the village square. We met the winemaker's wife. She comes from Macclesfield in England. She was handing out glasses for tastings and selling bottles of wine as well as looking after her four children. Her husband, the victorious wine maker, was celebrating elsewhere in a restaurant with friends. I asked her what happens in the village of Tour sur Orb.

'Well, there is a car boot sale in August,' she said.

We tasted her wines from the Domaine de la Croix Ronde, then walked round the small fair and admired a small alcohol still on wheels, which can transform 100 kilograms of fruit or grape juice into a brain-numbing drink with just the addition of fire and water. There was a clear liquid pouring out of a small copper tube into a large green glass bottle. We dipped our fingers into the liquid and licked them. It tasted good. Then we paid for lunch and sat down at a long trestle table covered with a white table cloth. We were served with a choice of paella or duck casserole, cooked in large metre round pans, a pichet of red wine, water and bread. Our fellow diners included two women who worked in a local shop; a man and his wife from Gignac, a town about half an hour's drive away; and the owner of the mobile still. I was struck by the uniformly good mood of the people in the courtyard. The sun was shining; there was plenty of wine and food and so there was every reason for people to be cheerful. But it struck me that this scene, taking place in front of a grand doorway of Renaissance proportions and beauty, is something that you would never find in England. It may be because there is very little local produce or community. Food is bought in supermarkets and nobody is too sure where it comes from. People avoid their neighbours, building huge hedges and fences to keep them away.

A girl wearing a cowboy hat came up and asked us if we wanted coffee. What I really wanted was to find a hammock and have a sleep under some trees, but coffee would be an acceptable alternative. We were still trying to get to Lodève. Matthieu, the owner of the mobile still, had finished his lunch and stopped to talk some more about the mechanics of maintaining a still. We contemplated making him an offer for his business. It struck us, sitting in the shadow of the château, that there could be worse ways to make a living in the Languedoc.

When we had drunk the coffee, we set off for Lodève, but got distracted by Lunas. Lunas is a sleepy town with a beautiful château that has been turned into a hotel restaurant and a wide lazy river that looks like it would be good for fishing. There are leafy trees by the river bank and stone bridges that span the river. We stopped by the river and sat on the bank looking for fish. When we woke up we determined to go to Lodève next year.

Last night we had a memorable evening, the kind that seems possible only here. We went to Château Coujan, possibly the most romantic spot in the entire region.

When you park the cars you are greeted by the screeching of peacocks, an impossibly exotic sound. History is everywhere, even underfoot. You are standing on a fossilised coral reef, for this part of the Hérault valley used to be under seawater. This is perhaps the only vineyard built on a reef. Where you park the car is the site of a Roman villa. The owners dug up a mosaic and put it in the 11th century Romanesque chapel. Across the courtyard is the 19th century château, masked partly by giant plane trees. There is a large building that houses the offices and wine storage. Beside that is the lodging where up to 70 grape pickers used to stay each harvest. Built almost on to the château is an enormous chai, that houses ten giant oak foudres either side of an aisle.

For once though we weren't here to taste wine but to listen to music. First, there was a buffet supper, with roast meats, pasta, melon, tomatoes doused in olive oil and basil leaves, bread and a fine selection of wines from the estate. The air was stifling. We sat inside what was probably an old stable, then went outside to a courtyard to listen to two flamenco guitarists. They had played two songs when the sky decided to join in. There was thunder, lightning and sudden heavy rain. It hadn't rained for three months, so the rain came as a relief. At first it was tempting to stand out in it, but it rained so hard, the water pouring off the roofs and forming rivers on the gravel, that people rushed indoors. The guitarists were just about to start again, when a bolt of lightning hit the château's electricity supply. Plunged into darkness, for once we were grateful for the smokers, who held up their lighters. Then candles were found, the musicians played and sang, and we drove home happy through the vineyards, singing and sighting wild boars playing in the rain.

Otherwise, how have things changed in the last three years? There are now more English drinkers in the bars than French ones. The camaraderie of a pint is something that the English seem to miss, so they gather and pass their time together. I see nothing wrong in this, although it is surprising when you go in a bar to find people discussing house prices in England and how much they still hate Thatcher. There are more cars on the road with foreign number plates and more new houses around the old villages. These are mainly full of French people from the north, escaping the flatness and the grey weather. Large suburbs of Paris are now empty and unnecessary. Everybody wants to come south. Now the room is ready for you, there is no excuse for you not to come, too. I think you will find you like it here. I am sure you will find much to make you grumble, too, but you would miss that anyway. A good grumble can be better than a cup of tea, as you always say.

Editor's note: Kitty never made it to the Languedoc. She died in hospital aged 97, too soon to watch her beloved Sussex Cricket Club pick up the County Championship for the first time in their long history. She is buried in the graveyard of St Mary's Church in Newick, Sussex.

SOURCES

Languedoc Méditerranéen, Christine Bonneton, Paris, 1989.

Lettres de mon Moulin, Alphonse Daudet, Paris, 1934.

In the Land of Pain, Alphonse Daudet, English translation by Julian Barnes, London, 2002.

Maillol, Bertrand Lorquin, London, 1975.

L'Eldorado du Vin, Les châteaux de Béziers en Languedoc, Jean-Denis Bergasse, Montpellier, 1994.

Between Meals, A.J. Liebling, New York, 1986.

Picasso, Patrick O'Brian, New York, 1994.

From Sea to Sea, L.T.C. Rolt, Allen Lane, 1973.

Ensérune, Martine Schwaller, Paris, 1993.

Le Pays Cathare, Jacques Berlioz, Auder, 2000.

The Albigensian Crusade, Jonathan Sumption, London, 1999.

Carnet du Littoral, Languedoc, Christiane Remblier, Paris, 1997.

Les Couleurs de la France, Jean Philippe et Dominique Lenclos, Paris, 1990.

The Death of Jean Moulin, Patrick Marnham, London, 2000.

INDEX

271

Index

Index